insideout

{insideout}
our stories, our faith in 40 devotions

CHAD EASTHAM

NATALIE GRANT

RACHEL HOCKETT

KJ-52

JENNA LUCADO

BRIE REED

KIMIKO SOLDATI

AYIESHA WOODS

THOMAS NELSON
Since 1798

NASHVILLE   DALLAS   MEXICO CITY   RIO DE JANEIRO   BEIJING

Published in Nashville, Tennessee, by Thomas Nelson. Thomas Nelson is a trademark of Thomas Nelson, Inc.

Thomas Nelson, Inc., titles may be purchased in bulk for educational, business, fund-raising or sales promotional use. For information, please e-mail SpecialMarkets@ThomasNelson.com.

Scripture selections from *The Holy Bible New Century Version*®, copyright © 2005 by Thomas Nelson, Inc. Used by permission.

Devotions in "Chad Eastham: Guys & Girls" are adapted, with permission, from The *Truth about Guys* by Chad Easham. Nashville: Thomas Nelson, © 2006 by Chad Eastham. All rights reserved.

Biographical information and devotions in "Natalie Grant: The Real You" are adapted, with permission, from *The Real Me: Being the Girl God Sees* by Natalie Grant. Thomas Nelson, © 2005 by Natalie Grant. All rights reserved.

Mark Moring's May 2, 2005, interview with KJ-52 quoted, with permission, from www.ChristianMusicToday.com.

Except as noted, biographical information is adapted and photos are used, with permission, from www.revolvetour.com, www.chadeastham.com, www.kj52.com, www.kimiko-usa.com, and www.ayieshawoods.com.

The photo of Natalie Grant is by Dominick Guillemot and is used by permission.

The photo of Jenna Lucado is by Karen James and is used by permission.

The photo of KJ-52 is used by permission of Paradigm Management Group.

ISBN: 978-1-4003-1097-5

Printed in the United States of America
08 09 10 RRD 6 5 4 3

{contents}

7. KIMIKO SOLDATI: EXCELLENCE

8. AYIESHA WOODS: SURPRISED BY GOD'S PLAN

{introduction}

what does your life revolve around?

hey, girlfriend, what's goin' on with you?

Actually, what's goin' *'round*?

Are you riding a happy merry-go-round of friends, school, family, and boys? Or do you feel like you're living inside a tornado that's tossing you around with a bunch of strange and scary stuff? Maybe you feel like you've been dumped on a desert island in the middle of a sea of circling sharks. Or maybe you're wrapped up in so many activities—sports and music and work and church friends and all sorts of other things—that you really haven't had time to stop and think about what's actually going on inside your head.

Whatever's going 'round with you right now, we want to help you look through all the flying debris and swirling emotions and find out what your life is *really* revolving around. What's at the center of your private, personal self? Is it something you can cling to when times are tough? Something that helps you chill when things are crazy? Something that brings you peace when your life totally stinks?

Or is it something temporary, something that seems important today but can melt into nothing tomorrow, vanishing like fog that disappears in the sunrise?

We've asked some awesome people to put together this little book of devotions to help you identify what your life revolves around. To find out—right now, right here—what's *really* most important to you. To help you get your head straight, your heart right, and your priorities in order.

These writers have been where you are. They know what it's like to ride a hurricane of thoughts and feelings, and they'll tell you straight on what they may have learned the hard way. They know what it's like to wear a happy smile that hides inside pain. They know what it's like when you're so busy you don't really *know* how you feel.

They'll make you laugh. But most importantly, they'll make you *think*. They'll help you get to know yourself, inside and out. And they'll lead you to the One who created you and longs to be at the center of your life.

One way to use this book is to begin at the beginning and work your way through it reading each writer's personal story on the weekend and then reading one devo a day during the week. Or open it anywhere and read a devo or personal story by a different writer each day, if that works for you. Whatever you choose to read, take a minute to let the words soak in; think about the Scripture verse and prayer each devo includes. Then record your own thoughts and responses in the journal pages provided.

We hope the ideas shared in these pages will inspire you to know and appreciate yourself the way God knows and loves you, inside and out. Then make sure your life revolves around *him*.

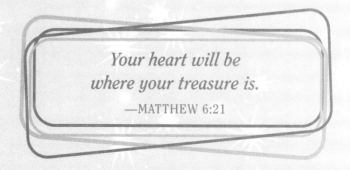

Your heart will be where your treasure is.
—MATTHEW 6:21

GUYS & GIRLS

{chad eastham}

Chad Eastham speaks nationwide as a youth culture expert about at-risk youth behaviors. He is the assistant director of Healthy Visions, an education-based not-for-profit organization. He knows what he's talking about, having experienced a lot of at-risk behaviors himself—drinking, drug abuse, encounters with police, actions leading to juvenile detention, and more. Chad has served with Campus Crusade for Christ; he's also worked as a chemical-dependency counselor and an Alaskan adventure guide. He's an advocate for youth issues nationally. He's also the coauthor of a national award-winning curriculum on sexual education for youth; his book, *The Truth About Guys*, gives girls honest answers to burning questions about the opposite sex.

{knowing where you fit in}

When I was a kid, my life revolved around being cool. Mom taught me that God and Jesus were important, but Jesus never stopped kids from making fun of me at school. He wasn't someone I could eat lunch with, and he never helped me with my homework.

The whole idea of God being love and truth didn't translate from the Bible into my real life. I needed people to like me, and I wanted to know that I wasn't a dork. My desire to fit in took precedence over acting like Jesus.

But as hard as I tried, I *wasn't* fitting in. I was angry all the time and saying all the wrong things. None of the girls I wanted to like me ever did, and I never quite made it into the "cool" circle. Obviously, something was wrong with me. I knew I wanted something better, but I didn't know what it was or how to get it.

Thanks to some bad choices and lousy life circumstances, I ended up in a detention center. Then, at age fifteen, I spent just over a year in one of the most intensive drug and alcohol treatment facilities in the country.

When I arrived in that dimly lit, padded security room, I felt like I had reached the end. It's funny, isn't it, how sometimes the beginning feels like the end.

Gradually my life changed. The people in that rehab center gave me something valuable—the hope that things could be different. They helped me realize I wasn't the only person who wanted to feel normal, accepted, and like I belonged.

I started believing I wasn't a piece of junk after all. For the first time in my life, God and Jesus made sense to me in real life. For example, Jesus said we're to treat other people like we want to be treated ourselves. Well, I started to see that kind of behavior as an opportunity to have good friends and to be nice to people.

I was sent out to talk with kids at juvenile detention centers and other places. I talked with them the way I wished others had talked with me before I messed up: I just tried to be real with them. I spoke to them in the language they were used to.

Now I know that God created me for a purpose. Now I know I'm someone who has made mistakes but is forgiven. Now I *know* I have value. After all, I was made in God's own image.

And so were you.

—Chad Eastham

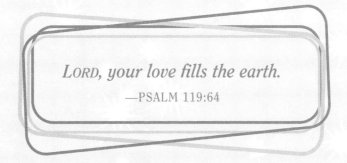

LORD, *your love fills the earth.*
—PSALM 119:64

who's who and whose

news flash: You get to decide who's in your life.

Well, most of the time, at least. You're still stuck with your pesky little brother or sister, no matter what, and let's face it: once your family's dog has bonded with you, you're doomed to wearing mutt fuzz on every piece of clothing you own.

If only you could get that awesome guy in your class to adore you the way Drooley the Wonder Dog does, right?

Maybe you're wearing the cutest clothes and the coolest makeup and you've done your hair in the latest style, but he's still ignoring you, and now you're wondering what else you have to do to catch his eye.

Actually, you can stop trying to figure out what kind of girl he finds attractive, because I'm a guy, and I can tell you right now. For starters, maybe it's a good idea to stop focusing on who Mr. Cool likes and instead figure out who you are.

Why? Because the truth is, guys like girls who like themselves. They're attracted to girls who know their own value—and know what they have to offer. In short, if you think you're great, so will he. What he thinks about you depends on what you think about yourself. This is one of the most important things I know to tell you. I haven't found a guy yet who disagrees with me.

I'm not talking about being conceited or vain or arrogant or snotty. I'm talking about simply being sure of your worth because you're sure of the One who created you—and it is obvious he doesn't make

> You made my whole being; you formed me in my mother's body. I praise you because you made me in an amazing and wonderful way.
> —PSALM 139:13–14

junk. When you know both *who* you are and *whose* you are, it shows in the way you live your life. And that confidence, that attitude, becomes a strong, positive magnet that attracts others to you. It's what makes you lovable.

That's how you get to decide who's in your life and how you're treated. If you don't think much of yourself, you'll create an impression that causes others to respond with the same attitude: they won't think much of you either. But if your life shows others that you *know* you're a marvelous creation, a treasure, a child of God, then others will be attracted to your confidence and want to be around you.

God made each one of us unique and beautiful. Your job is to make sure you're treated in a way that's respectful to you *and* to your Creator.

Dear Heavenly Father,
Thank you for loving me. Thank you for creating me. Help me learn to love and appreciate the unique person you made me to be. And please forgive me when I fail to recognize all that is amazing and wonderful in me. Thank you for the gift of life. Help me to use it to honor you. In Christ's name I pray. Amen.

insideout

{ write from the heart }

Think about the qualities God created in you that make you uniquely *you*. List them here and describe how you're currently using them— and how you might use them more effectively—to live your life for him.

_____

_____

_____

_____

_____

_____

_____

_____

_____

_____

_____

_____

Eleanor Powell said, "What we are is God's gift to us. What we become is our gift to God." See yourself the way God sees you. Don't depend on friends or family to set your value; God has already done that. Let his love shine through your life . . . and into others.

could i have a do-over?

have you ever done something stupid in front of a lot of people? And do you wish now that you—and all those other people —could please, please, please just forget it ever happened?

Hmmmmm. Let me think. Yes, I seem to recall that happening to me . . . a few dozen times.

> **God will yet fill your mouth with laughter and your lips with shouts of joy.**
> —JOB 8:21

One of the stupidest things I ever did was my (unfortunately) unforgettable performance at a high school talent show. The rap artist Vanilla Ice had a big hit back then called "Ice, Ice Baby." I decided that, even though I'm a white guy who can't dance or sing and should know better than to try, I would give a personally choreo-graphed performance of "Ice, Ice Baby" at my school's talent show.

It was impressive, in a tragic sort of way. I did an awesome Running Man for about a minute. Then I improvised with some high-stepping, arm-flinging gyrations that probably caused most of the audience members to start thinking, *Hey, this is getting creepy.*

Then came my grand finale. I'd planned a back-flip springy kind of thing that would ignite the crowd with wild applause. So as the lyrics came to a close, I "white-guy danced" my way over to a big mat with the school's mascot printed on it. I got down in a squat and pushed off for the back flip. I don't really know what happened next, but apparently the mat slipped, and instead of landing on my hands, I actually landed on my head and knocked myself clean out!

It would have been better if I could have remained unconscious for a couple of hours, but nooooo. I came to as the guys were carrying me out—so I got to hear the audience doing their own little rap: "Get some ice, ice, you little baby."

Yeah, it was stupid. But it was funny too. And remembering it now reminds me of how God uses even our stupid mistakes to bring us close to him—and bring others close to us. I have told this story a few times when I speak to audiences of young people around the country, and it always makes them laugh. It also tells them, *Hey, I'm one of you. I do stupid stuff. I make mistakes. But God helps me make things right again. That's what grace and forgiveness are all about.* (Plus, anything dumb you do makes a good story later. Tuck that one into your pocket.)

Gracious God,
Your love and forgiveness are precious gifts that give me courage to keep trying when things get tough and the odds are against me. I'm not afraid to try because I know you're with me. When I fall you're there to pick me up and help me start over. Thank you, Lord! Amen.

insideout

{ write from the heart }

What's your most embarrassing experience in front of others? Is it still too painful to think about, or are you finally able to laugh about it? How can you help relieve others' discomfort when they make mistakes and do something stupid?

_____

_____

_____

_____

_____

_____

_____

god never promised us life would be easy. He promised to be with us throughout our life. When you make a mistake, when you've done something stupid, feel God's loving presence carrying you through the anguish and embarrassment. Ask him to help you dry your tears and find a way to learn from—and laugh at—your mistakes.

relating through differences

*g*irls and guys are different.

Now that I've impressed you with my amazing wisdom and astonishing intellect, please let me offer an insightful example gained through my personal and, uhh . . . , scientific observations.

Girls and guys say hello differently. You can tell how excited girls are to see each other by the pitch of their voices and the ear-piercing way they shriek their words: "Oh my GOSH! I'm so GLAD TO SEE YOU! Girl, you look so GOOD, and your outfit— I could just DIE!"

When I first started speaking at gatherings of teenage girls, like the Revolve conferences, I kept thinking someone was getting hurt. Now I know it's just that you're excited to see each other.

In contrast to girls, guys greet each other with very little emotion: "Hey, what's up?" We don't shake hands. We do a thing like we're in some kind of gang initiation: a knuckle-bump, wrist-grab, thumb-twist, finger-flip ritual while we say stuff like,

> In the Lord women are not independent of men, and men are not independent of women. This is true because woman came from man, but also man is born from woman. But everything comes from God.
>
> —1 CORINTHIANS 11:11–12

"How you doin', bro?" "Just tryin' to live, dude. Just tryin' to survive another day, you know what I'm sayin'?"

Okay, it's kinda dumb. It's actually really dumb. But so is screaming your head off because you're so glad to see your girlfriend who has just returned from the restroom.

The fact is, neither way is wrong. It's just different. It's the way God made us. He created us as individuals with unique

personalities and appearances while also placing us in groups with general similarities and mutual tendencies.

He designed us to live in relationship with one another, to hang out with each other. And learning to understand and appreciate our differences, as well as our similarities, helps those relationships thrive. It helps us be friends who understand each other and value each other's unique, God-given characteristics.

Heavenly Father,

Thank you for designing me as a unique creation. Please help me see and appreciate the unique qualities of your other creations as well. Show me how to speak and listen in ways that help me relate to my friends and family so that your love flows through me to them. In Jesus's name, amen.

insideout

{ write from the heart }

Think about the different ways you and your friends talk and listen to each other. What kinds of communication styles do you see in yourself and others? How can you use that awareness to become a better communicator?

_____

_____

_____

_____

_____

_____

_____

_____

Everyone has a unique style of communicating, but some people have a special way of encouraging us to share our thoughts and feelings. Think of someone you know who's easy to talk to. Have you ever thought about what a valuable gift it is to you, having him or her as a good listener in your life? What can you do to be a better listener for your friends and family?

like spaghetti and waffles

So let's talk some more about talking. Come on. You know you love to talk. After all, you're a girl. You can talk about anything and everything—and do ten other things *while* you're talking. To us guys, girl talk can be amazing—and very confusing. I sometimes describe the difference between the way we communicate by saying girls are like spaghetti and guys are like waffles.

Guy talk is compartmentalized, like the little squares on a waffle. We tend to focus on one idea at a time. Now we might talk about cars. Later we might talk about pizza. Tomorrow we may discuss video games. This is oversimplified, but I think you can get the point.

In comparison, a single conversation among girlfriends can easily flow through a tangle of topics from friends to outfits to food to rainy days to pets to homework to boys to hairstyles to . . . I almost get a nosebleed just trying to keep up with some of the girls' conversations I've overheard. It's even worse when I'm expected to participate.

The other day I got lost in one of those conversations with my friend Maggie. I didn't understand what was happening as she bounced from one topic to another without even taking a breath. Nothing was making sense to me. I explained to her—nicely, thank you—that my mind has an easier time staying on track with one idea at a time. I wanted to listen, but I couldn't follow her train of thought because it seemed scattered and random to me while it made perfect sense to her.

She was great about it. She slowed

> After three days they found Jesus sitting in the Temple with the teachers, listening to them and asking them questions.
> —LUKE 2:46

down, stayed on each topic. I could tell she was trying to talk so my brain understood more clearly. I could appreciate what she was saying, and she seemed to enjoy learning a little something about how my brain worked.

We've already agreed on the obvious fact that God made guys and girls different. He created us to relate to each other. Sometimes just learning about our differences—learning how the other person hears our words clearly—can help us do that.

Dear Jesus,
You are the Son of God, the Creator of all things, yet you took time to listen to others, to show interest in what they had to say, and to question them about their ideas. Help me be more like you in everything I do, including being a good listener to my friends and family. Amen.

insideout
{ write from the heart }

Describe a time when you felt someone was really listening to you.
Then write about a time you tried talking to someone who was
distracted by things happening around you. How did you feel
differently in each of those situations, and what can you learn about
listening from remembering those occasions?

_____

_____

_____

_____

_____

_____

_____

Someone once said the greatest gift we can
give someone is to listen, understand, and care.
How does it make you feel when you're trying to
share your innermost thoughts with someone
and he or she "listens" while watching a TV
show or playing a video game? How can you tell
someone is really listening—and how do you
give that gift to others?

15

Sometimes girls are weird. At least they seem that way to guys. To us, *weird* means *different*, and situations that are different can feel strange to us—uncomfortable and unfamiliar.

A lot of guys think that being around girls means heading into unfamiliar territory. But even in unfamiliar places, we can find very cool things. For me, one of the coolest things has been having good girl friends: girls . . . who are actually real friends.

You already know this because you're a girl, but for guys it's a lightbulb moment to realize that friends who are girls actually see us for who we are. Too many teens and adults get caught up in the dating game, with both partners trying to be someone or some*thing* they're not so they can impress the other person—who's doing likewise.

There's something really different (there's that word again) about how guys look at girls as dates and how we look at them as friends. Ironically, when I'm looking at a girl as a potential date, most of my attention is on me, me, me, maybe because I want her to see me as the attractive guy. On the other hand, when I'm looking at a girl as my friend, my focus is more about noticing all the *real* stuff about *her*: her intelligence and insight, her sense of humor, how comfortable it feels to just hang out with her and share stories, laughter, and feelings.

> I call you friends, because I have made known to you everything I heard from my Father.
> —JOHN 15:15

Girls are created for intimacy. You can reach out and connect with your guy friends in a way that's comforting to us. Sure, it feels different, but mostly it feels safe.

The truth is this: what a guy wants most in a girl is a friend. It really is. Well, the *right* guys at least. But that's who you're wondering about . . . right?? Friends change you and challenge you and inspire you. The basis of any good relationship is friendship; friends care enough to be honest with you. More than that, friends know your faults and like you anyway. We all want that. Real friends put your needs above their own wants. Learn how to be a friend, and a lot of other stuff falls into place. Nothing weird about that!

Dear Jesus,

You sought out friends while you lived on earth, just as we do today. You celebrated their happy times and wept with them when their hearts were broken, just as we do with our friends now. Thank you for the wonderful gift of friendship. Please show me ways to share this gift with others who may be lonely and sad. Let your kind and loving encouragement flow through me to them in friendship. In Jesus's name, amen.

insideout
{ write from the heart }

How are your friendships with girls different from your friendships with guys? If you've been in a dating situation, how did that experience differ from a friendship experience? In which situation are you more comfortable? More real? Why do you think that is?

_____

_____

_____

_____

_____

the Bible is a great place to see what real friendships look like, and also how friendships can be restored after they're damaged by thoughtless mistakes. Read the story of Job in the Old Testament to see how **not** to be a friend. Then consider all the mistakes Simon Peter made as Jesus's friend and follower and how Jesus repeatedly forgave Peter and valued him as the "rock" on which Christ's church would be built. (Read Matthew 14:22–33, 36–46; Matthew 26:69–79; John 18:10–11, 13–27; and Matthew 16:18.)

THE REAL YOU

{natalie grant}

Natalie Grant recorded her first album in 1999. Since then there have been more albums and an impressive collection of Top Ten radio hits, including her number one hit song "Held."

Despite her acclaim as a popular Christian singer and songwriter, Natalie struggled with a poor self-image that pushed her into a destructive eating disorder. Now recovered after years of fighting bulimia, Natalie shares her story with audiences around the country, reminding girls that "true self-worth isn't based on what others feel about you . . . [but] on how God sees you. You are only who God says you are. And God says you are wonderful."

Natalie was named Female Vocalist of the Year at the Dove Awards ceremony for both 2005 and 2006. She and her husband, music producer and band leader for the Revolve tour Bernie Herms, live in Nashville with their twin daughters, Grace Ana and Isabelle Noelle.

{finding jesus in an unlikely place}

i grew up in a loving home filled with five children and two parents who gathered each night at the dinner table. With the kind of loving, nurturing, affirmative background I had, it's hard to explain what happened to me at a very early age.

I became an obsessed people pleaser. I was always trying to please everyone—my parents, teachers, siblings, friends. My value totally depended on what other people thought of me.

During college, and then as my music career got going, I stayed so busy impressing everyone around me that I lost sight of who I really was. I became bulimic, secretly enduring an endless cycle of eating and then making myself vomit.

It's hard to understand why anyone would fall victim to such a strange and disgusting habit, but millions of people do, and most of them are young girls. For me, throwing up felt like a way of gaining control and battling my feelings of insecurity.

My healing began, strangely enough, in a bathroom somewhere after I'd once again made myself throw up. When you hear Christians say God meets us where we are and accepts us as we are, you might think it always happens in church. It doesn't. On the day my healing began, I felt the presence of God as I lay on the cold, dirty floor curled around the base of a toilet.

Suddenly I sensed his presence. It was as though he'd been standing beside me, gently holding my hair back as I leaned over the toilet. I sensed him whispering in my ear, *You're better than this. I created you for more than this.*

I'd like to say I got up from there and was miraculously made whole and never made another mistake. But that would be a big fat lie. Recovery is a process. Day by day, the more I discovered and understood who God says I am—that I am created in his image—the more I understood his love for me. Today I can truthfully say God has healed me, and I am so grateful.

—Natalie Grant

I will be with you always.
—Matthew 28:20

what does God expect of you?

When I step onto a concert stage, I know a lot is expected of me. First, people in the audience are probably expecting me to sing, because, well, that's what I do. They probably expect me to remember the lyrics and stay on key and share my music in a way that makes them think or feel good or come closer to God.

Oh, and they probably expect me to *not* fall off the stage, which, believe it or not, I did one time in Iowa. I tripped over a monitor and took a nosedive right into the audience.

When a lot is expected of us, we feel a lot of pressure, don't we? We want to impress those around us with our abilities, our personalities, our character. We want people to like us.

Nothing wrong with that, really. We all like feeling loved and appreciated. But when our desire for others' approval becomes the main thing our lives revolve around, we're riding the wrong merry-go-round!

When we let others determine our sense of value, *our* sense of worth changes as *their* opinion of us changes. When we fall off our pedestal of perfection (or a concert stage) and they call us losers—we believe them! We think, *Yeah, they're right. I'm an idiot.*

Instead, we need to believe what our Creator calls us. He calls us his own child. He says we're the best thing *ever*. And most amazing of all, he expects us to live our lives with the confidence that we are created in his own image—and who's gonna call *him* a loser?! Not me!

> Then God said, "Let us make human beings in our image and likeness."
> —GENESIS 1:26

Eternal God, Creator of everything—Creator of me,
Thank you for loving me and valuing me and forgiving me, no
matter how far I fall. Help me remember always that I am
your child, cherished and loved, and that no one else's opinion
of me matters as much as yours. And no matter what, you
think I'm wonderful. Amen.

Martin Luther said, "God does not love us
because we are valuable. We are valuable
because God loves us." How does your opinion
of yourself change when you remember you
are a child of God, created in his own image?

insideout

{ write from the heart }

Think of a time when you failed—or at least didn't do what others expected of you. How did their words and opinion affect you? When one of your friends messes up big time, how can you reach out to him or her?

_____

_____

_____

_____

_____

_____

_____

_____

_____

_____

_____

_____

_____

_____

_____

the magazines lie

It was like a scene out of a movie. I had arrived at the California setting for my first professional photo shoot. The photographer was there, of course, along with the stylist, the manager, the director, and the makeup artist. Wow! I never knew a girl needed so many people just to have her picture taken.

As the center of all that attention, I felt like a real star—until everyone started talking about me as if I weren't there. They said things like, "We can use these pants to make her look taller and this light to make her look thinner and this angle to diminish her round face." And of course my freckles had to be hidden.

At one point the makeup artist said matter-of-factly, "Wow. You have large pores. But hey, that's what Photoshop's for. Whatever I don't clear up they can airbrush out on the computer."

After twelve grueling hours of being poked, prodded, and painted, the charade parade finally ended and what few morsels of positive self-image I might have started out with that morning were long gone.

Later, I was amazed at the beautiful girl in the "finished" photograph. Her face was flawless, not a freckle in sight. Every pore had been resized; every blemish had magically disappeared.

> Truth will continue forever, but lies are only for a moment.
> —PROVERBS 12:19

I couldn't take my eyes off her. But who was she? The photo experts had not only airbrushed my face; they had airbrushed away a little piece of my soul. I looked at that photo and felt like a liar. *People will think that girl is me,* I thought, *but it's really not.*

The world expects us to be something we're not. It wants us to think we can't measure up without the top-name makeup, the expensive hairstyle, the designer clothes. The world tells us, *You're not good enough.* The fact is, the world is lying. We don't need that stuff to make us feel loved and valued.

That's why it's important to spend more time studying God's Word and less time admiring those "perfect" beauties in magazines. While the magazines tell us we have to buy what they're advertising if we want to be good enough, God tells us we're adorable and beautiful just the way we are. Just the way he made us.

There's a big difference between God and the glamour-biz gurus.

The difference is, God doesn't lie.

Dear God,
When I stand in front of my mirror, help me see myself through your eyes and know myself as you know me. Help me be the real me, the girl you created, instead of wishing I were the airbrushed image the world wants to create. Amen.

insideout
{ write from the heart }

Look at yourself in the mirror through God's eyes and describe what you see. Record your descriptions here, and after each characteristic, write what the Bible says God saw when he looked upon you after he created you: "It was very good" (Genesis 1:31).

_____

_____

_____

_____

_____

_____

_____

_____

there's nothing wrong with looking good! It's natural for a girl to want to experiment with clothes and makeup and hairstyles and make herself attractive. Just make sure you don't lose the real you in your pursuit of worldly beauty. Don't obsess over what shows up in your mirror. It's the stuff that shows what's in your heart that counts.

what really matters

my friend Agnes would be the first to admit she's been a people pleaser all her life. She remembers thinking, as a child, *If I could just be a better girl, maybe Mom wouldn't be so worried all the time. Or maybe Daddy wouldn't work so much.*

In her teenage years, that thinking translated into her constant struggles to be one of the cool girls the boys would pay attention to. She became what she thought they wanted.

In college, she became an over-achiever, killing herself for an A+ because an A simply wouldn't do. Seriously.

Agnes is a smart girl—but it still took her a long time to see that devoting her whole life to pleasing others is a waste of time and effort. Now she understands that what other people think of her has little to do with the kind of life God created her for.

In Ephesians 4:17, when the apostle Paul talked about "those who do not believe," he said, "Their thoughts are worth nothing." When we spend more time trying to live up to others' expectations than we do in getting to know what God created us for, our lives get sucked up in an endless vacuum.

God didn't make us so we could spend our lives desperately seeking other people's approval and acceptance. He didn't create us for a life of insecurity and fear. We weren't placed on this planet to be people pleasers. We are accepted and loved by the One who created us. Nothing else matters

> But we speak the Good News because God tested us and trusted us to do it. When we speak, we are not trying to please people, but God, who tests our hearts.
>
> —1 THESSALONIANS 2:4

except giving that love back to him by loving and caring for others, just as we love and take care of ourselves. When we do that, we please God. And pleasing him is what's important.

Dear Heavenly Father,
I want to be the girl you created me to be. Give me the wisdom to trust that you knew what you were doing when you made me the way I am. Help me love myself as you love me—and live in a way that shows that love to the world. In Jesus's name, I pray. Amen.

the real you isn't perfect. Don't exhaust yourself pretending to be someone you're not!

insideout

{ writing from the heart }

You weren't placed on this planet to please yourself. You weren't even placed here to please others. So why are you here? To please God. Think of things you can say and do that show your life revolves around pleasing God, rather than people. How could your relationships with your friends and family be strengthened if you resolved to live your life for God?

there's a saying, "If you haven't gone through hard times yet, just hang on—your time's comin'!"

Just being a teenager is hard enough most of the time, with all those swirling hormones that can make you feel like an emotional yoyo. But for some of you, life's even tougher right now. It may seem like life's bad guys are throwing rocks at you while you're already down in the pit.

Maybe you've experienced a death in your family. Or things are really messed up at school. Maybe your parents' marriage is falling apart. Or you didn't get accepted by the college you wanted. Maybe your best friend has moved away. Or your parent or your sibling has been sent to the war zone. Maybe you're feeling down and you don't even know why.

Whatever your circumstances, remember what God promised. He promised to be with you in the hard times and the dark moments of your life. He promised never to leave you or forget you. He promised to remember your name and love you forever. He has a plan for you. He created you for a purpose. And he's gonna help you get through the thing that's troubling you now so that, with his help, you can achieve that work he has for you to do.

Hang on to those promises when life knocks you into the pit. And in that dark place, believe that he is with you, feel his love embracing you, and rest in his amazing strength.

> God has said, "I will never leave you; I will never abandon you."
> —HEBREWS 13:5

I'm in a hard spot, Father, and I need your help to get through it. Please stay near me. Help me feel your love enfolding me and your strength sustaining me. Help me to climb out of this pit and live out the plan you've created for me. In your Son's name, I ask it. Amen.

think about being in a totally dark room, maybe a windowless closet with no light at all. Then imagine yourself striking a match and lighting a candle. Think about the change that one little flame makes in that darkest of places. That's what a little flame of faith can do in the dark times of your life. It doesn't remove the darkness, but it helps you find your way out of it.

insideout
{writing from the heart}

What's the most difficult thing in your life right now? How do you sense God's presence? How do you see yourself a month from now? A year from now?

_____

_____

_____

_____

_____

_____

_____

_____

_____

_____

_____

_____

_____

_____

_____

_____

_____

_____

showing the world a real christian

don't you just love the look on people's faces when they find out that the coolest person in the room is a true Christian? You don't have to be a mind reader to know the confusion that's rippin' through their heads: *Get outta here! That great guy (or that amazing girl) is a Christian? Man, there's no stinkin' way. That kid is way too cool to be one of those goody-goody Jesus people.*

A lot of people out there expect Christians to be nerdy-looking geeks wearing last century's styles and up-tight attitudes. Seriously! They think of believers as super-religious, boring, no-fun freaks. I want to be just the opposite. Isn't it fun to show them that Christians love to laugh and enjoy life just like everybody else?

I want to radiate such contagious joy and joyful enthusiasm that other people want what I've got—and that's the love of God and the gift of salvation. Just thinking about it now gives my spirit a boost!

We don't have to go around preaching a list of dos and don'ts. Being a *real* Christian means being Christlike. Which means loving people. Serving them. Living a life of compassion. Treating others as we want to be treated.

Real Christians know what it means to be *in* the world, but not *of* the world. We can be trendsetters, inside and out, by looking our best while also setting an example of how to live a godly life.

> Do not be shaped by this world; instead be changed within by a new way of thinking. Then you will be able to decide what God wants for you; you will know what is good and pleasing to him and what is perfect.
> —ROMANS 12:2

Dear Father,

Thank you for the precious gift of your Son, Jesus. Help me be more like him in everything I do and say and think. Fill me with so much of your joyful love that it overflows onto those around me and brings us all closer to you. In Jesus's name, amen.

When we put God at the center of our lives and make him the focus of everything we do, his love radiates through us like gravity, pulling others into orbit around him too.

insideout

{ write from the heart }

Has there been a time when someone has been pleasantly surprised to find out you're a Christian? Or, knowing you are a Christian, was disappointed to find out that you would be doing something shockingly wrong? Write about those times and list the words that describe how you felt—and how you think the other person felt as well. And remember: the world watches you.

_____

_____

_____

_____

_____

_____

_____

_____

_____

_____

_____

_____

_____

_____

BEING GOD'S GIRL

{rachel hockett}

Rachel Hockett's music career started at the age of three as she traveled the country with her gospel-singing parents, Billy and Sara Gaines. She later shared a Dove Award for Inspirational Album of the Year with her parents for a project called "Generation to Generation."

Later, when her parents' music-ministry career required them to be away from home a lot of the time, Rachel took on the responsibility of seeing that her two younger brothers were well cared for, even when an adult caregiver was present.

The pressure to be constantly responsible during her preteen and teenage years pushed Rachel into an attitude of perfectionism that led to health problems during her early adult years. Today she credits her husband, Brian, with helping her acknowledge her problem and seek professional help. His support helped her stay strong in her faith and pure in their relationship while they were dating.

A graduate (with honors!) of Western Kentucky University, Rachel currently teaches voice and movement at a Christian school and day care and also performs with her longtime friends Kara Tualatai and Amanda Omartian in the musical group Prelude.

{letting go of perfectionism}

a little voice in my head started whispering lies to me during a lonely and unsettled time in my life. My parents had moved to another state, but I had stayed behind in the city where I'd grown up so I could continue college. My brothers, who had often been my responsibility while they were growing up, were living on their own in a different part of town. It seemed so strange to not know what they were doing every minute, to no longer be in control of their lives, responsible for their safety and well-being.

I didn't know how to handle this sudden change in what occupied my mind. It was as if I needed something new to worry about now that my brothers were no longer my responsibility.

It's hard to understand exactly how it happened, but gradually, I started thinking I had to be perfect at everything: the way I looked, the way I sang. I thought I needed to be the perfect daughter and sister and have the perfect home and the perfect life. Those were the little lies that started to fill my head.

Eventually those mental lies so completely consumed me that I developed some habits and behaviors that threatened my health and sent me into depression. It was Brian, now my husband, who finally pushed me to seek professional help. At first I refused to listen to him. Now I thank God he persisted. With Brian's encouragement and the help of God and some caring professionals he put in my path—and also through the use of medication—

I am letting go of unhealthy perfectionism and making my way back to being the girl God created me to be.

Going from sickness to wholeness isn't like walking through a door. It's a continuing journey, and not always an easy one. But God is with me, Brian loves me, friends and loved ones are praying for me, and my life is now full of hope—and honesty.

—Rachel Hockett

My hope is in you, so may goodness and honesty guard me.
—PSALM 25:21

make the call

In the early years when Mom and Dad were traveling for their musical performances, my brothers and I stayed home with adult babysitters. But even with a babysitter present, I took on the responsibility of enforcing the rules, remembering the schedule, and keeping the household running smoothly.

One weekend, when I was eighteen and was babysitting my brothers while our parents were out of town, my youngest brother wanted to go skateboarding with some guys I didn't know but had heard about. This little brother was the rebel of the family. He kept me on my toes!

I didn't like the skateboarding idea, but he was insistent. Finally, I said, "Let's see what Dad says."

We called Dad, and I spoke first, laying out the situation as objectively as I could. Then my brother launched into his arguments: It wasn't a big deal. It was just skateboarding. He wouldn't be gone all day. They were good guys—people just talked trash about them, that's all.

"Well?" I asked Dad. "Can he go or not?"

"You're in charge, Rachel," Dad answered. "You make the call."

Me? Make the call? Can't you just do it? After all, you're the parent.

It would have been so easy to say yes. My brother would have slapped me a high-five and happily headed out the door. But I knew that, as the one in charge of my brother's safety and well-being—as the one making the call—I had to say no.

My brother was furious, but I stood my ground. I knew it was the right thing to do, and I knew Dad would back me up. That gave me the courage to be strong.

> People who do what is right may have many problems, but the LORD will solve them all.
> —PSALM 34:19

Sometimes it would be so easy to give in, to go along with the crowd. But knowing what's right—and knowing the One who's standing behind us and empowering us to know right from wrong—gives us courage to make the call, and to be the girls God wants us to be.

Dear Jesus,

By both your words and your life on earth, you've shown me what is right. Thank you, Lord, for helping me know the truth. Please give me the courage to follow your example, even in difficult circumstances. Help me make the call and do what is right. Amen.

A Christian's journey is full of joy, but the trip is never easy. What brings you joy in spite of difficulties? What gives you courage to do what is right when others choose a different path?

insideout
{ write from the heart }

Write about times when you have done what is right when it would
have been easier to go along with the crowd. What happened as a
result of your decision? When have you taken the easy way out?
Describe the differences in those two experiences.

_____

_____

_____

_____

_____

_____

_____

_____

_____

_____

_____

_____

_____

_____

brian and I met in church. He says he saw me and thought, *Who is THAT?* I saw him and thought, *Ohhhh, he's so cute . . . but not my type.*

A girlfriend of mine who also knew Brian suggested that the three of us go bowling. I sat in the front seat of his car and flipped through the radio stations like I already knew him. In hindsight, I see how comfortable I was with him, right from the start.

Our friendship grew in the following months. He says he wasn't thinking, *I want to be your boyfriend* but, *You're a good person. I want to get to know you.*

I started thinking, *He's gonna make some girl a really good catch.*

A year later, when I was eighteen, he gave me my first kiss. By then we had become such good friends, we hadn't even realized we had fallen in love.

That one kiss led to another, and it easily could have led to more than that.

Fortunately, God helped us realize what was happening: our hormones were threatening to take control of us! God also gave us strength to do the right thing.

> Women of Jerusalem, promise me by the gazelles and the deer not to awaken or excite my feelings of love until it is ready.
> —SONG OF SONGS 2:7

We came to an agreement. As hard as it was, we mutually agreed that we would cut out the romantic kissing completely, because we could see that it was leading us into dangerous territory. And we both agreed that we wanted to have the relationship God intended for us: one that kept us pure, that postponed sex until we were married.

It wasn't easy. But we were very determined. We wanted to be able to tell our own teenagers someday, "We stayed pure. It wasn't easy, but we did it. And you can do it too."

Dear Jesus,
Help me keep myself pure and my relationships wholesome so that I honor your plan for my life and live as the girl you want me to be. In Jesus's name, amen.

Sometimes doing the right thing means resisting super-strong temptations. Ask God for the strength you need to do his will—especially when you're tempted to do something else!

insideout

{ write from the heart }

What temptations have you faced—or are you facing now—that
cause you to turn to God for strength to resist them? What are the
good things that might come out of this stressful experience?

_____

_____

_____

_____

_____

_____

_____

_____

_____

_____

_____

_____

_____

_____

_____

_____

_____

_____

_____

brian and I dated for four years before we were married. Uh-huh. That's right: *four years*. And we kept our relationship pure all that time. It wasn't easy. But neither is earning a college degree. Or learning how to snow ski. Or sharing the gospel.

The truth is, God gives us the strength to do what he *wants* us to do (see Philippians 4:13). He also gives us helpers so we don't have to struggle alone through the day-to-day nitty-gritty of doing his will.

> ## Love is patient.
> —1 CORINTHIANS 13:4

Brian and I loved each other a lot. But we loved God even more. And we knew we wanted to save sex for the confines of marriage, because that's what he expected of us. So we developed a "plan of action." First, we agreed to be totally honest with each other in identifying the behaviors, gestures—and anything else— that might cause our minds to wander off course . . . and eventually lead our bodies into trouble.

Next, we called our youth pastors and said, "We need help."

They said, "Come on over."

We agreed to meet with them once a month and go through any problems we were facing in our relationship. They prayed with us, encouraged us, and armed us with knowledge and with biblical insights that inspired us to stay strong in our faith—and in our goal of staying pure. They stressed that if one of us was pressuring the other to do something physical, we weren't showing love to each other, but selfishness. And they reminded us that the first virtue of love is *patience*.

We went through premarital counseling, which helped even more.

And then, *finally!* we were married. And oh, how glad we were that we had waited.

No, it wasn't easy, the choice Brian and I made. But the struggle we endured for a short time was well worth the reward we'll enjoy for a lifetime . . . and beyond.

Dear Jesus,

I want to be a girl who shows, by everything I do and every relationship I have, that I love you more than anything or anyone and that I am guided by your will and your teachings. Please give me your strength in the face of temptation and your patience in times of trial. In your name, I ask it. Amen.

just as exercise sometimes hurts as it's strengthening our physical muscles, life experiences can stretch us painfully as they strengthen our spiritual muscles and help build our endurance to do God's will.

insideout

{ write from the heart }

Write out a "plan of action" you might take in meeting a challenge you're facing, whether it's at school or in a relationship. Whom could you ask to hold you accountable as you work your way through your plan?

_____

_____

_____

_____

_____

_____

_____

_____

_____

_____

_____

_____

_____

_____

_____

It was the morning of my grandfather's funeral, and I lay in bed worrying about the tragedy the day would hold.

No, not the tragedy of grieving over my grandfather's death, but the anxiety about the way my funeral dress fit. I wanted it to fit perfectly. Isn't that sick, to be so self-centered? Isn't it amazing how selfish and narrow-minded we can be when we let something besides God's love for us fill our minds?

I knew that dress would fit a little tighter than it had the last time I wore it. *I'm gaining weight,* I thought. *I'm getting fat.*

And then it happened. A different thought came into my head, one that had to have come straight from our loving God. *Stop focusing on your clothes and how you look! Focus on the One who created you to be just the way you are. Focus on what's important right now.*

What was important that day was coming together with my family to honor my grandfather. Suddenly my mind skipped to the story I'd heard all my life about how he had been a raging alcoholic before I was born. But when he learned I was on the way, he went to Alcoholics Anonymous, on his own, without pressure from his family. You see, he wanted to be sober so that he could spend time with me, his granddaughter. He wanted to be a good influence for me, so he got sober—and he stayed sober the rest of his life.

The memory made me smile. I dried my tears, got out of bed, and put on the dress. Yes, it did fit a little tighter than it used to, but instead of letting that thought consume me, I focused instead on how blessed I've been to have a grandfather—and a God—

> You are worried and upset about many things. Only one thing is important.
> —LUKE 10:41-42

who loved me before I was even born. They must have thought I was really special!

If you're wallowing in a bed of anxiety and self-pity right now, remember you're loved too and ask God to redirect your thoughts. Then get up and get going. Go out there and be God's girl, a special creation clothed in love.

Dear Jesus,
Lift me up when I'm wallowing in self-pity; broaden my vision when I'm focused only on myself. Help me to see myself as you created me and be the girl you created me to be. Amen.

What does your world revolve around? If it's the image in your mirror, you're tracking on the wrong orbit, girl! Fill your mind with reminders of Christ's love for you, and step out as his representative on earth.

insideout
{write from the heart}

Write about your priorities today—If it's evening, describe how you spent your day. If it's morning, describe how you plan to spend your day. What is your biggest concern right now? Do you need to shift your priorities?

when God stepped in

The old saying "Experience is the best teacher" is never truer than when we're feeling down, or we're stuck in some situation that seems like a miserable prison.

For me, that's when the lessons of past experiences kick in. And I know right where to find them. I go back and read my journals.

> But let those who follow you be happy and glad. They love you for saving them.
> —PSALM 40:16

Mom taught me to journal when I was just a little girl. Now, when I go back and read my old journals, I see the progress I've made as I've learned the freedom God's love gives me.

My earliest journals are filled with descriptions of constant fears and thoughts of failure, my sense of never measuring up to God's expectations. "God, I'm so sorry I did that," I wrote again and again. Or, "God, I feel like you're not happy with me." Or, "Lord, please make me a better daughter (or sister or friend)."

But as I keep reading my journals, I see the days when God stepped in. For instance, one day when I was in the middle of writing, "God, please show me how to be a better Christian. Show me what to do for you," I also wrote that a strong thought came into my head. It felt as though God were saying to me, "Rachel, until you really understand how much I love you, all that you're *doing* isn't really for me. It's for your own sense of accomplishment. You don't have to do everything perfectly. You don't have to do anything to *earn* my love. I've already given it to you. All I ask is that you love me back. Then, if you do my work, do it simply because you love me and nothing more."

After that day, I see my journals reflecting an increasing joy in all my activities and a growing sense of my value. For example, one day I simply wrote, "Thank you, God, for letting me see my favorite flower today. That was so nice of you!"

Now, if a dark day comes, I know the darkness won't last. I've got proof right there in my journal. God has been there for me in the past, and experience has taught me he'll step into my life today and every day to help me be the girl his love empowers me to be.

Dear Lord,
Whenever dark times imprison my mind, please remind me of your love that sets me free, and guide me back to the light again. In Jesus's name, amen.

God's love gives us comfort, and his grace gives us courage. Even when we make mistakes, we're loved unconditionally and renewed when we ask to be forgiven.

insideout
{ write from the heart }

Write about some lessons you've learned through experience. Sometimes these are lessons we've learned "the hard way." Other times, they're things we've learned by experiencing the love and support of someone whose guidance and advice warned us away from a difficult or dangerous experience.

IN THE SPOTLIGHT

{kj-52}

KJ-52 is an unlikely rap star. After all, as he describes himself, he's "a white kid from South Florida who loves hip-hop and used to drive a minivan." Even more unlikely, he's an unabashed follower of Jesus Christ who says his goal is "to share my heart with anyone who will listen."

And a lot of people *are* listening. He has won four Dove Awards, including three awards for Rap/Hip Hop Album of the Year (in 2004, 2005, and 2007) and Recorded Song of the Year for 2007.

As his career has soared, KJ—whose real name is Jonah Sorrentino—has become one of the most respected names in Christian music as a songwriter, producer, minister, and comic poet.

Many of KJ's songs are drawn from his life experiences, including the emotional pain resulting from his parents' divorce when he was nine, and the anger he struggled to hold in check during his teenage years. Now he refuses to dwell on the past. As he told a ChristianMusicToday.com interviewer, "I'm going to move forward because God is going to give me the strength to do that."

{taking a stand}

When I was about fifteen, I was hanging out with some neighborhood friends at the home of a kid whose dad was a pastor. The pastor had put up a large cross on the front lawn of their house.

These guys thought up this "fun" thing to do. They began to mock Christ by climbing up on the cross and pretending to be crucified, laughing hysterically while they acted out their disrespectful drama.

I had made a commitment to Christ a few months before, but I wasn't really attending a church, and I had no Christian friends—except maybe the pastor's kid, and he wasn't exactly the best role model. That day he was climbing on the cross with everyone else.

After the crucifying got old, one kid found a football in the yard and launched it toward the cross. The others all took their turn at "passing practice," using the cross for a target.

When they handed me the football, for a split second I didn't know what to do. I stood there feeling totally alone. Should I go along with my friends—or take a stand for my newfound relationship with God?

I dropped the football and walked away.

"Why didn't you throw it?" one of the kids called after me.

"I'm not stupid," I yelled over my shoulder. "I know what's important."

That day I realized God meant more to me than what my friends thought.

He still does. Being a Christian means I have to take a stand every day. I'm not going to let the world influence me. Instead, I'm doing my best to influence the world for Christ.

—KJ-52

> *I am not ashamed of the Good News,*
> *because it is the power God uses*
> *to save everyone who believes.*
> —ROMANS 1:16

no more debating

Before I came to know Christ, I was incredibly skeptical of who God is. There was a kid in my ninth-grade class who was a believer, and I made it my personal quest to prove to him that God wasn't real and that his faith was false. We argued constantly and debated each other endlessly. I was determined to prove that I was right and he was wrong. I wanted so badly to be "one up" on God.

Just one year later, when I was fifteen, I hit rock bottom. Maybe you've been to rock bottom too. I was a "normal" teenager who looked fine on the outside but was full of anger inside. I was mad about my parents' divorce, mad about my current situation, mad about everything.

Anger was the one steadfast thing in my life that was otherwise empty of feeling. But then, in that vacuum, guess what started creeping in: those arguments the dorky ninth-grade debater guy had tossed at me.

Finally I decided, *What have I got to lose?* I cried out to God. I remember praying, "God, if you're really who they say you are, prove it to me, and I'll follow you for the rest of my life."

Have you ever heard someone say they prayed a prayer like that and instantly their pain eased, their broken heart healed, their skin cleared up, and their teeth got straight?

Me neither.

It doesn't happen that way.

But it does happen. As I began to read the Bible and study what it meant to have faith, the reliability of God's Word and the truth of who God is gradually became real for me.

There's no more debating it: I know God is real. When I hit rock bottom, I landed on the Rock.

> LORD, you are my Rock, the one who saves me.
> —PSALM 19:14

Dear God,
Thank you for believing in me even when I didn't believe in
you. Thank you for proving yourself to be as real to me as
you are faithful. In Jesus's name, amen.

What have **you** got to lose
by believing—or not
believing—that God is real?

insideout

{ write from the heart }

How would you "debate" a nonbeliever if you were called upon to
do so? Write what you might say that would convince someone God
is real.

_____

_____

_____

_____

_____

_____

_____

_____

_____

_____

_____

_____

_____

_____

_____

little gifts multiplied, big sins forgiven

People are always asking me where my professional name comes from. The KJ comes from my old rap name, which was King J Mack. (The J is for my real name, Jonah.) The 52, pronounced "five-two," is a reference to the Bible story that tells how a boy gave Jesus his lunch of "five loaves of barley bread and two little fish" and Jesus blessed that little bit of food and fed more than five thousand people with it (see John 6:1–14).

Like that boy in the Bible, I gave Christ a little: I was a white guy from Florida who wanted to do Christian rap. I didn't have a lot to offer, but God made something big out of it.

And God not only multiplied the good stuff in my life, he also subtracted the bad. I made some poor choices when I was a teenager. I did some stuff I wasn't proud of, including bullying kids when I thought I could get away with it. I remember, in particular, giving this one kid a hard time—and an atomic wedgie . . .

> It's true that you did wrong, but don't turn away from the LORD. Serve the LORD with all your heart.
> —1 SAMUEL 12:20

After I came to know Christ, I felt a lot of guilt about my past behavior. But the more I studied God's Word, the more I understood what his unconditional love and total forgiveness are all about. I came to see that if God can take my little bit of talent and turn it into something big, then I'm gonna give God the glory with every word I sing. If God can take away my sins "as far as the east is from west" (Psalm 103:12), if he can forgive my mean, messed-up life and turn it into something good, then I need to learn how to forgive, too, when someone does something I don't like.

God didn't do these things once and turn me loose. He multiplies my little gifts and forgives my big mistakes every day. And that is how he changed my life forever.

Lord Jesus,
Thank you for the miracles you perform in my life every day.
Remind me always to give my little talents to you . . . and
help me forgive others the way you have forgiven me. Amen.

God gives us all gifts. What are you doing with **yours**?

insideout

{write from the heart}

List the gifts God has given you, and thank him for each one of them. Now list some of the mistakes you've made. Ask God to forgive you for each of them, then draw a line through them, reminding yourself that God has taken them away.

_____

_____

_____

_____

_____

_____

_____

_____

_____

_____

_____

_____

_____

_____

_____

_____

_____

day three with kj-52
for the ladies

as I was doing research for my album *Behind the Musik*, I began to notice how much hip hop music was geared toward girls. The concepts, the lyrics, the imagery . . . it was all packaged to appeal to *you*.

Yet there was also something really strange about it. Even though the total package was aimed at girls, what was actually being portrayed about girls by the lyrics and images in mainstream hip hop songs and videos was incredibly negative.

Then came the saddest thing: realizing that the majority of hip hop music is bought by girls—which means that not only are they buying the music, they are also buying into the negative imagery about girls.

The next surprise was examining Christian hip hop and finding nothing that challenged those negative images of the mainstream lyrics.

Since no one else seemed ready to step up and sing about what God has to say about girls, I figured . . . hey, I'm cool. I should be the one.

The result was my song "For the Ladies." It's dedicated to my beautiful wife, and it talks about how totally awesome godly women—the ones who make Jesus number one in their lives—are.

> She is strong and is respected by the people. She looks forward to the future with joy.
> —PROVERBS 31:25

When I demo-ed the song, I got some flak. After all, while hip hop music is aimed at girls, it's also a male-driven, macho-fueled genre, and it's deemed "soft" to portray anything to the contrary. The "experts" urged me to drop the idea.

But I knew I needed to take a stand. And, not to brag or anything—okay, I'm braggin'—the response has been *huge*.

I constantly hear from girls telling me, "Thank you, KJ!"

And I'm pleased to answer, "You're welcome, ladies."

Father God,

Creator of male and female, help me to respect myself enough to stand up for what's right and to turn away from whatever disrespects your creation. Thank you, Lord, for making me who I am. In Jesus's name, amen.

the Bible tells us to fill our minds and hearts with "things that are good and worthy of praise" (see Philippians 4:8). What are **you** listening to?

insideout
{ write from the heart }

Write the lyrics of a popular contemporary song that you like. Do the lyrics show respect for you as a girl? Are they "good and worthy of praise"?

_____

_____

_____

_____

_____

_____

_____

_____

_____

_____

_____

_____

_____

_____

_____

_____

standing strong in the face of criticism

If you've been a Christian very long at all, you know that taking a stand for Christ isn't always easy. In fact, it's *rarely* easy! Let the world know you're a Christian, and you open yourself up to a whole lot of criticism, especially if your work puts you in the spotlight.

For me, that criticism occasionally gets ugly, especially when other rappers write songs that diss me or when music critics condemn me because I'm a Jesus follower.

The worst criticism came after I released a song called "Dear Slim" that told another rapper, the superstar known as Eminem, I was praying for him to tone down his violent lyrics and think about his impact on young fans. The next thing I knew, VH1 ranked me number twenty-six on their forty "least hip hop moments." I was ridiculed on national TV in front of millions of people because I took a stand for what I felt God wanted me to do.

It wasn't my favorite thing in the whole world, you know what I'm sayin'?

But I had two choices for how to respond: I could do what my human nature wanted me to do—or what God wanted me to do.

> You have heard that it was said, "Love your neighbor and hate your enemies." But I say to you, love your enemies. Pray for those who hurt you.
> —MATTHEW 5:43–44

The Bible says we're to pray for those who wrong us and love the ones who criticize us. So, rather than returning the favor and dissing those people back, I've asked God to help me forgive them, and I pray for them every day.

Meanwhile, something really interesting happened. After hearing about my song on national TV, many people were curious,

and they decided to check it out. Apparently a lot of them liked what they heard because my Internet message board immediately lit up with some awesome messages. I especially liked the one that offered a tip about how to handle non-Christians. I can't use the exact word here, but it basically said, Love the heck out of 'em.

Dear Jesus,
Thank you for the opportunities you've given me to proclaim my love for you. Help me see those who ridicule me as your children too, in need of your love. Amen.

a wise person has said that what doesn't kill you will make you stronger. When you face criticism for your beliefs, stand strong, knowing God is standing with you.

insideout
{ write from the heart }

Write about a time when someone hurt your feelings or made you angry. Describe how you responded—as human nature wanted, or as God wanted.

_____

_____

_____

_____

_____

_____

_____

_____

_____

_____

_____

_____

_____

_____

_____

_____

_____

seventh-grade romance

In seventh grade, my life revolved around girls. Especially *one* girl, Jenny. Man, she was awesome!

But girls did scary things with their hair back then. They took their bangs and made 'em stand up about two feet above their foreheads. It looked like a rat got on top of her head and built a nest. I'm serious. It was scary!

> Remember to love me always because you are good, LORD.
> —PSALM 25:7

I know it's hard to believe, but I wasn't exactly what you'd call cool back then. I was five foot two and had a size 12 foot. I looked like an L. I wasn't the smartest kid either, but I had one great talent: I knew how to write a note to a girl.

I wrote Jenny this great note. It said, "Will you go out with me? Check yes [I put

a huge box beside *yes*] or no [teensy box for *no*]."

I sent it to her in class via the sneeze technique: Ah-*choo*! I tossed the note backward over my head toward Jenny. Wam! It stuck right in her bangs.

She untangled the note, made a mark on it, and tossed it back.

She said yes!

That night I called Jenny on the phone. We talked about nothing for three hours.

Seriously—nothing: "Whaddaya doin'?"

"Nuthin'. Whadda *you* doin'?"

"Nuthin'."

That's how you went out back then.

The next day I saw Jenny in the hallway. I reached up to put my arm around her. It's seventh grade, and she's, like, a foot taller than me—plus the bangs. So I had to stand on tiptoe and reach *really* high.

She knocked my arm right off her shoulder!

70

Shocked and confused, I stood there wondering what was going on while I tried to get my shoulder back in its socket. Later Jenny wrote me a note. It said, "Can we just be friends?"

Back then, my world revolved around girls. Today my world revolves around something even cooler: God, the *Creator* of girls . . . and guys . . . and every other great thing.

How about you? What does *your* world revolve around?

Thank you, dear God, for loving me with a love that never ends. Amen.

remembering that God loves us unconditionally makes it easier for us to show Christ's love and patience to others, even in trying situations.

insideout

{ write from the heart }

Write about the love you've shared with others: parents, siblings, friends, or that special boy. How does each kind of love feel different? And how are they all different from God's love?

FAMILY

{jenna lucado}

If your dad is America's leading inspirational author and the "Best Preacher in America," according to *Reader's Digest*, does that mean that life at your house is perfect? Uh . . . maybe not, says Jenna Lucado.

Jenna was born in Brazil while her parents were missionaries there. She grew up as a preacher's kid in San Antonio, Texas. Her dad, Max, preaches at Oak Hills Church and has also written dozens of books on Christian living. The rest of the Lucado family includes mom Denalyn and younger sisters Andrea and Sara.

Jenna graduated from Abilene Christian University with a degree in public relations. Now she's back home in San Antonio, starting a new career. But this phase at home will be slightly different from the days when the three Lucado sisters blared Celine Dion upstairs and fought over the remote. The family dinner table back then was never silent, except for quiet Dad, whose only words usually consisted of asking someone to pass the butter. God knew that Max had the perfect combination of gentle leadership and sensitivity for an estrogen-dominated home.

{always a winna}

the campaign trail looked smooth. Nothing stood in my way of becoming senior class president. Well, nothing except one minor detail: my opponent, Nathan Wiley.

My strategy was simple. I would exploit his top three weaknesses by magnifying my top three strengths, as follows:

Wiley's weaknesses	My strengths
1. He was a boy.	1. I was a girl.
2. He was smart.	2. I had personality.
3. He was a brunet.	3. I was blonde (at the time).

Piece of cake! I had this election in the bag.

Totally unconcerned about the actual voting, I was already practicing my victory speech as the entire school filed into the cafeteria for the announcement of the winner. I was just about to stand up and accept my new title when the principal announced, "Congratulations, . . . Nathan Wiley, the new senior class president!"

What?! Nathan Wiley?

That "one minor detail" had won the election. Although my friends quickly reached out to comfort me, I shamefully skipped lunch to avoid the stares and ran to my car, calling the only person I knew who would empathize with my misery: Mom.

Driving home, I needed windshield wipers for my tears. But when I pulled into our driveway, a rainbow of color on the front lawn caught my water-logged eyes. Tied to stakes stuck in the grass, a bright, twenty-foot-long sign was stretched across the lawn proclaiming, "Jenna is a Winna."

Mom and Dad were waiting for me just inside the door. I rushed into Dad's arms and soaked his shirt with my tears. I felt so humiliated, so defeated.

Dad reminded me that I would always have his vote in every race I ran, that I would always be number one in his eyes, and that, win or lose, no matter what, he loved me.

Do you sometimes feel humiliated and defeated too? Do you have days when you need windshield wipers for your tears? Maybe you need to be reminded that your Father loves you, win or lose, no matter what.

You may feel defeated by the world. You may believe you aren't as pretty as she is. Or that you aren't as smart as he is. But like a proud father, God has painted a sign that says, "I love you." He promises that you'll always be number one in his eyes; you'll always be a "winna" to him.

—Jenna Lucado

> *From far away the* LORD *appeared to his people and said, "I love you people with a love that will last forever."*
> —JEREMIAH 31:3

manna from God, moses . . . and mom

We were no longer the Lucado kids. We were the Israelites. And Moses (formerly known as Dad) had called us out of Egypt (the TV room) to the Promised Land (family devotion time).

At our house, family devotions sometimes meant "doing" a scene from the Bible. I was eight years old when Dad helped us reenact a scene from the Exodus. He led us through the desert (the kitchen and dining room), reminding us that he was Moses and we were the children of Israel and that we weren't surrounded by furniture and cabinets full of food but by endless hills of blowing sand.

Eventually we got to the living room— I mean, the wilderness—and with a little prompting from Mom, we cried, "We are hungry, Moses! Is God not going to feed us?!"

So Moses prayed to God on behalf of the complaining Israelites, asking for food. Opening his eyes, Dad gave a brief nod in Mom's direction. She flipped a wall switch,

and Nilla Wafers flew off the blades of the ceiling fan. Manna from heaven!

I still can't look at Nilla Wafers without thinking of the Exodus—and of that night when Moses and Mom reminded us again that God's blessings sometimes come from unexpected places (even ceiling fans).

> When the dew was gone, thin flakes like frost were on the desert ground. . . . Moses told them, "This is the bread the LORD has given you to eat." . . . The Israelites ate manna for forty years.
> —EXODUS 16:14–15, 35

Dear God,

Thank you for the gifts you give us, beginning with the gift of family. Help me to see the blessings you sprinkle upon my life, and to share them with others. In Christ's name, I pray. Amen.

how can you live out a Bible lesson so that others see the blessings God gives his children?

insideout

Describe some of the blessings that have come into your life just when you needed them most. Can you be "manna from heaven" to someone who's going through a desert right now?

_____

_____

_____

_____

_____

_____

_____

_____

_____

_____

_____

_____

_____

_____

_____

_____

_____

sharing battles . . . and regrets

In the Lucado home, we were taught to share from an early age. Given our background, you might think peace and harmony prevailed in the Lucado household and that the three PKs (preacher's kids) who lived there would graciously share their blessings with each other.

But you'd be wrong.

Our fiercest fights were over sharing. And the two wildest warriors were my sister Andrea and me:

Two years apart + same size = closet catastrophes.

Hoping to maintain peace, we created a Clothing Constitution:

1. If something was new, the original owner got to wear it first.
2. You had to ask before borrowing something. And the answer needed to be *yes*.
3. When complimented on a borrowed item, the borrower had to attribute the good taste to the rightful owner

(in other words, don't take credit for somethin' that ain't yours).

We also argued about who got to sit in the front seat every morning when Dad drove us to school. So Dad established a rule: Andrea would sit up front on odd-numbered days, and I got the even days. The rules helped but didn't stop the fights.

> When you see someone who has no clothes, give him yours, and don't refuse to help your own relatives.
> —ISAIAH 58:7

Looking back, I see that in our immaturity, we just weren't selfless enough to let the other person enjoy something. I hate to admit it, but I still struggle trying to "be happy with those who are happy," as Romans 12:15 tells us to do. I tend to care more about my own happiness than the happiness of others.

But my *biggest* regret now is not that I didn't share my clothes or the front seat, but, more importantly, that I didn't share my time. The priority list was as follows:

me, my friends, *then* my family. I regret not sharing dreams, not sharing struggles, and not sharing laughs with the two girls I love most in this world.

Sisters won't always live right down the hall.

Dear Jesus,
Thank you for the amazing love you've shared with me and the many blessings you've given me. Help me to share my possessions, myself, and my heart with others as I live my life the way you taught me to. Amen.

insideout
{ write from the heart }

When you think about sharing, what comes to mind? How has someone shared something valuable with you? What have you shared with those around you?

_____

_____

_____

_____

_____

> Often the greatest gift we can give to another person is the gift of our time as we share experiences, learning together, or when we listen from the heart.

_____

_____

_____

_____

_____

learning despite winning

I'm guessing you've developed some very strong negotiating skills. I sure did when I was a teenager. In what we called the Lucado Family Court, my sisters and I would present our well-thought-out arguments for everything from swimsuits to curfews while "the judges," our parents, carefully considered our pleas and presentations.

> God will always give what is right to his people who cry to him night and day, and he will not be slow to answer them.
>
> —LUKE 18:7

My greatest victory in family court came when I successfully argued an appeal of my parents' rule about dating. I was fifteen, and they had established a "law" that I couldn't date until I was sixteen. At the time, I was dying to go out with a senior named Mark. He had light blue eyes and a smile that made my knees go weak.

My argument (which I presented brilliantly, if I do say so myself) was, How am I going to be any different when I'm sixteen than I am now? A year won't make that big a difference.

Amazingly, Mom and Dad caved. They let me go! I was so excited that night when Mark came to pick me up. He passed the parental inspection and inquisition with flying colors, and off we went.

But guess what? The fairy tale date didn't end with a "happily ever after." I never dated Mark again, and I didn't even ask to date anyone else until I was sixteen.

Mom and Dad never said, "We told you so." Instead they prayed for God's perfect will to shadow my will as well as their own. Though I may have won one of the most compelling arguments in Lucado history, I learned that my desires can never beat the desires of what God has for me.

Father God,
Help me to know what's right—but also to understand that when things don't go the way I want them to, you may be teaching me a life lesson. In Jesus's name, amen.

a jokester once defined parents as "something so simple even a child can operate." Sometimes when we think we're getting our way, we may be heading into a lesson that shows us what God's way really is!

insideout

{write from the heart}

Is there something you're "negotiating" with your parents now?
Some exception to a rule you hope they'll make? Write your
arguments here—and also write the responses you expect to those
arguments. Whatever decision is reached, consider how God may
be using it to bring you wisdom and enlightenment.

_____

_____

_____

_____

_____

_____

_____

_____

_____

_____

_____

_____

_____

_____

_____

_____

don't you just hate it when your parents say the same thing over and over and *over*? Every time you hear those words again, you may roll your eyes and shake your head, irritated and exasperated by their all-knowing remarks.

At our house, one of those frequently repeated lines was my mom's infamous remark, "Nothing good happens after midnight."

Every time I heard it, my lips tightened and I thought what a ridiculous statement it was. *What difference does it make what time it is?*

I schemed to get around my parents' curfew rule any way I knew how so that I could experience those after-midnight hours with my friends. It was exciting to be out so late. Some of the best parties didn't start until 11 p.m., and even then, my friends and I wanted to dramatize our entrance by showing up as late as we could.

I never thought Mom's nagging words would ever prove true until I started noticing something eerie. As the night goes on, *everything* gets darker. Sure, physically, the night blackens and your vision weakens, but have you ever noticed that mentally, your thoughts darken and spiritually, your morals loosen? Alcohol seems less dangerous; a boyfriend's pressures seem more justified. Inhibitions leave . . .

It wasn't until *after midnight* that I

> I am sure that neither death, nor life, nor angels, nor ruling spirits, nothing now, nothing in the future, no powers, nothing above us, nothing below us, nor anything else in the whole world will ever be able to separate us from the love of God that is in Christ Jesus our Lord.
> —ROMANS 8:38–39

meddled with alcohol. It wasn't until *after midnight* that we trashed the front lawns of ex-boyfriends. It wasn't until *after midnight* that I noticed myself acting like someone I was not. I avoided my parents more. But as Mom's words kept echoing through my head, I felt ashamed of my new nighttime identity.

Eventually I confessed what I had done. As a result, privileges were lost, and repayment was arranged. But through it all, Dad told me the same thing over and over again: "Jenna," he said, "there is *nothing* you can do that will make us love you any more or any less."

Funny. That's the same thing our Father in heaven says over and over. And I don't know about you, but I never, *ever* get tired of hearing those words.

Dear Jesus,
In the darkest places of my life, help me feel your love surrounding me and keeping me strong in the face of challenges and temptations. Amen.

insideout
{write from the heart}

What are some of the things your parents say most frequently to you? Can you imagine yourself saying the same thing to your children someday? How would you say things differently to achieve the same purpose or impart the same guidance?

_____

_____

_____

_____

_____

_____

_____

_____

One of the most amazing discoveries for many young people is realizing that their parents were right all along. Have your parents done something "right" lately?

_____

_____

_____

One of my most vivid high school memories is also one of my hardest. I said something ugly about someone behind her back. My words were so cruel, it's hard for me now to believe I said them. But I did.

My cutting remarks quickly made the rounds of our school and got back to the girl I'd gossiped about. She confronted me and threw my words right back at me in front of my friends. I ended up writing out an apology and reading it to the lunch table of friends, my voice trembling as I sobbed out the words.

Despite that hard lesson, my tongue still gets me in trouble sometimes. I've been blessed with the gift of gab, and sometimes I "gab" without thinking. Either unintentionally or thoughtlessly, I say things that are hurtful and mean-spirited. My tongue is my fiercest weapon.

During my first year of high school, I hung out with kids who weren't Christians. I refused to get involved in our church's youth group; I lied to my parents, snuck out of the house a few times, messed around with alcohol, and more.

When things really started getting bad, I took a step back and realized I didn't want to continue on the dark path I was walking. I confessed to my parents everything I had done, and they listened lovingly.

> LORD, help me control my tongue; help me be careful about what I say.
> —PSALM 141:3

Dad opened up to me and shared some of the temptations he had struggled with when he was my age. Mom sat beside me, wrapped me in her arms, and cried with me. And once again, they assured me of their unconditional love.

The "L word" is used a lot in my family.

"I love you" rolls easily off the tongues of my parents and sisters and me at all times and in all circumstances. I've learned the hard way, if you're going to have the gift of gab, *this* is the thing to gab about. Gab about love.

Dear Heavenly Father,
Your Word is the Bible, and it speaks life and guidance into my heart. Help me be a girl who shows by her words, as well as her actions, that she is your girl. In Jesus's name, amen.

Mark Twain said that the difference between the right word and the almost right word is the difference between lightning and a lightning bug. Remember, before you speak, how powerful your words can be.

insideout
{write from the heart}

Consider how often you hear and use the "L word." What's the difference in hearing it from a family member and a friend? How does it make you feel to hear it? To say it? Is it hard for you to say? Why?

INSIDE OUT

{brie reed}

Australian-born Brie Reed is a passionate worship leader, songwriter, author, and speaker who holds a deep desire to reach people for Christ in a real and relevant way. She's also the host of the Revolve Tour.

Brie has been in ministry more than half her life, since joining her church's worship team at the age of twelve. She was a founding member of Australia's top-rated Christian kids touring group Rocfish and spent four years performing with them across Australia and New Zealand.

In addition to being a spokesperson for the Revolve Tour, she teaches singing, dancing, and acting classes and leads an after-school Bible study for teens. In her spare time, she continues to write music, lead worship at her local church, and share her love for God at various speaking and worship-leading engagements around the country.

{ surviving what i prayed wouldn't happen }

growing up in a wonderful Christian home, my brother, my sister, and I learned at an early age that the most important thing in life was a personal relationship with Jesus. We didn't own a TV until I was ten, so we spent a lot of time as a family playing Bible games, talking about Bible lessons, reading Bible stories, and staying busy at our church.

With such a spiritual background and idyllic family life, you have to wonder what caused me to sit on a beach one day and pray a very specific prayer: "God, whatever happens, don't ever let my family break up."

That was the one thing I thought I couldn't handle in my life. But it seemed so far-fetched, I almost laughed at my own words. It would never happen to my family.

But my biggest fear became a reality; when I was eighteen, my parents divorced. I can't even describe the pain I felt. Why had God allowed this to happen to me?

But even as I cried, night after night, and accused him of abandoning me, another unexpected prayer filled my heart: "Lord, use me. Use *this*. Give this pain a purpose and help me reach out with your love to others going through this nightmare. Help me show them you are real and you are faithful."

Soon after my parents got divorced, I found myself sitting at a café with a close friend. She wanted to talk because she had just found out her parents were splitting up too. It was one of those experiences where I was able to say, "Kate, I understand exactly what you're going through. It's hard and it hurts . . . but you'll get through it." I knew exactly how she felt that day as she sat there across from me . . . fighting back tears. But I couldn't have given Kate hope, or said the things I said with such influence, if I'd never experienced it myself.

I know God has a plan for everything, and I've learned to trust him no matter what.

—Brie Reed

Trust the LORD with all your heart.
—PROVERBS 3:5

have you ever walked into your bathroom thinking everything's okay, but then you look in the mirror and see the biggest, most disgusting zit in the middle of your forehead? Eeeuuwwww! You use every cover stick, concealer, and pimple product you have, but no matter how much you try to fix it, that thing just won't go away.

If you can relate to this, then we have a lot in common! Throughout high school, I had terrible skin—sometimes my face seemed completely *covered* with pimples. I was embarrassed and I hated it, but there wasn't much I could do to get rid of them.

I remember staring into the mirror one day feeling a bit depressed. There was a big football game that night, and all my friends would be there—including a guy I was interested in. I should have been excited, but all I could think about were the three massive new pimples on my chin.

Growing up, my parents had always told me I was beautiful, inside and out. They constantly reminded me that I was created in God's image and that true beauty came from within. I shouldn't spend so much time worrying about my outside appearance, they said.

That night before the game, I spent a few minutes feeling sorry for myself. Then I thought, *Brie, you are so much more than this! You're so much more than what you see in the mirror . . . so get over it!*

> Charm can fool you, and beauty can trick you, but a woman who respects the LORD should be praised.
> —PROVERBS 31:30

Since then, whenever I look in the mirror, I try to see myself from God's perspective. God thinks I'm beautiful. After all, he created me—pimples and all. And if he thinks I'm pretty, who am I to argue?!

Father God,

Thank you for loving me, no matter what. Please give me eyes to see myself as you see me: a beautiful girl, inside and out. In Jesus's name, amen.

Jesus told us to love our neighbors as ourselves . . . which means we're to **love ourselves**. How do you show love for the girl God created you to be?

insideout

{ write from the heart }

When you think about how much God values and cherishes you,
how does that make you feel? Compare how *you* see yourself—and
how God sees you.

the audition

there were thirty of us guys and girls at the all-day audition. We were trying out for a new Christian performing group for Australian kids, and it was the scariest day of my life—sort of like *American Idol* but condensed to one day. Six judges sat at a table and asked us to do various things to demonstrate our talent.

First we had to sing a song we'd chosen. Then we had to sing harmony to another song they chose (I got "Twinkle, Twinkle, Little Star").

Next, one of the judges said, "Dance for us like you're dancing in the bedroom with no one watching." (I thought, *You've got to be kidding.*) That became one of the most embarrassing moments of my life.

Then, after doing some drama exercises, we had to pretend to be newsreaders, reading three different news articles out of the local paper. At the end of the day, they split us into groups of four and made us choose a new song to perform—with only five minutes to practice. It was full-on!

Later that night, I received a phone call from one of the judges telling me I'd made the group. I was so excited, when I got off the phone I screamed! I was so relieved to know I'd measured up to the judges' expectations.

It stills amazes me to think how hard I had to work that day to be accepted as a member of Rocfish, which became the number one Christian performing group for kids in Australia and New Zealand. We went all over the country presenting high-energy,

> You have been saved by grace through believing. You did not save yourselves; it was a gift from God. It was not the result of your own efforts, so you cannot brag about it.
> —EPHESIANS 2:8–9

laughter-filled programs that shared the gospel through song, dance, and drama. And we had a lot of fun doing it.

But here's something even more amazing: to be accepted by God as a member of his family, all I have to do is . . . show up! I don't have to do a song and dance to meet his expectations. I don't have to pretend that what I'm doing on the outside doesn't hide what's inside my heart. All he expects of me is that I acknowledge him and love him. And for me, those are very easy things to do!

Dear Father,
Thank you for loving me unconditionally. Thank you for the gift of your Son. Help me to discover the other gifts you have given me and to use them in ways that honor you. In Jesus's name, amen.

insideout

We don't have to audition to be accepted by God (thank goodness!), just believe in his Son. But what could you do to show God how much you love being in his family?

> god gives each of us different talents. You might have a hidden gift within you, just waiting to be revealed to the outside world.

day three with brie
making the most of every day

i try to be patient. Really I do. But it's definitely something I've struggled with from time to time.

As a teenager, one of the things I felt most impatient about was knowing what my future was going to be like. *What will I do when I finish school? Who will my closest friends be? Where will I live? Who will I live with? Will I ever get to travel? Will I marry? Who will I marry? How many kids will I have?* I was *so* impatient for the future to arrive, because I wanted to know *all* the answers! It was as if my body was living in the present while my heart and mind were focused only on the unknown future.

During that time, I started keeping a journal and writing down what God was teaching me every day. Now, as I read back through my journals, I see that, more than anything, God was teaching me patience. I also see that he wanted me to put my attention completely on him—and I finally got the message. On July 16, 2004, I wrote, "I'm understanding what you're telling me, God . . . that I need to be satisfied in you alone."

I started to enjoy every day more by focusing on the blessings in my life *today*. I would wake up and think about whatever plans I had for that specific day—going to the beach with my family, hanging out with friends on the weekend, going to church, doing some kind of musical activity. I learned to be completely satisfied with my life *at that point*, knowing I was where God wanted me to be that day.

> Be joyful because you have hope. Be patient when trouble comes, and pray at all times.
> —ROMANS 12:12

100

I (finally!) realized there's no point in stressing about the future. I became determined to enjoy the journey and not worry so much about the goal at the end!

When I look at my life now, I see how faithful God has been to me in the past. He's given me more than I could have ever hoped for. I'm so glad I've learned to put my trust in him for my future.

Thank you, dear Jesus, for the lessons in patience that you teach me, and thank you for the rewards that come when I listen to you! Amen.

life is about the journey.
Not just the destination.

insideout

{ write from the heart }

As you think about the past year of your life—and perhaps as you reread your journal—what lessons do you see God teaching you? Write them here.

_____

_____

_____

_____

_____

_____

_____

_____

_____

_____

_____

_____

_____

_____

_____

_____

_____

_____

planes, trains, and bibles

Only about 4 percent of the population of Australia are active Christians, which means 96 percent are not. So for me, growing up as a Christian in Australia was almost like being a missionary in my own country!

When I was in high school there, I rode part of the way home on a public train. Sometimes I'd pull my Bible out of my bag and start reading, and people would look at me like I was some kind of weirdo.

They were obviously judging me harshly by what they saw me doing, and sometimes I almost felt scared that one of them might start bothering me or attacking me or something. Once a lady sat down next to me, and when she saw my Bible, she got up and moved to another seat!

In America, it's not so unusual to read a Bible in public, but occasionally I'll find myself reading it on an airplane, and I'll sense the person in the next seat mentally moving away from me. Maybe people are afraid I'll start preaching at them!

I love reading the Bible, and I want to be able to study Scriptures whenever I feel like it. I don't want to stop reading it in public just because it might make other people feel uncomfortable. But on the other hand, I don't want people to feel like they need to avoid me either. It would have been great if Biblezines were around back when

> The LORD laughs at those who laugh at him, but he gives grace to those who are not proud.
> —PROVERBS 3:34

I was a girl riding the train in Australia. They're basically a Bible that looks like a modern-day magazine. They're great, and so practical; they probably wouldn't have offended people the way my Bible did.

The whole purpose of my reading the Bible is to get to know God more, and I

want to help others get to know him more too. We're so blessed to have immediate, easy access to God's Word wherever we are and wherever we go. Whether it's reading the Bible on your laptop when traveling or having a verse-a-day program that text-messages your cell phone, there are so many options available. It's good to be constantly reminded that God himself is with us too, wherever . . . *forever.*

Dear Jesus,
Thank you for the freedom to learn more about you through your Word. Help me to use your teachings to share your love with others. In Jesus's name, amen.

insideout
{ write from the heart }

Where do you most enjoy reading your Bible? Where do you feel awkward doing it? What can you do to make other people more comfortable if they see you reading God's Word?

_____

_____

_____

_____

_____

_____

_____

helen Keller said, "We could never learn to be brave and patient if there were only joy in the world." How do challenges and difficulties make you a stronger, braver Christian?

_____

_____

_____

_____

_____

_____

coming from a different place

I've been in America almost three years now, and I'm still amazed at how different it is from Australia. One of the first things that surprised me was how many American businesses have drive-throughs. You can stay in your car and do your banking, order dinner, drop off laundry, pick up prescriptions, get your oil changed . . . basically do almost everything. It's amazing! We don't have that in Australia.

Your cheese is totally different from ours. Most of your cheese seems to be white—or a seriously bright orange. Ours is yellow. I was scared to eat American cheese when I first saw it, but now I'm used to it.

And you have different names for things. You call green peppers, . . . well, green peppers. In Australia, we call them capsicum. I know, weird, hey? (And that's another difference: Americans are more inclined to end a sentence with "ya know?" than "hey?")

One of my *favorite* things about America is the shoes, because shoes are *so* cheap here, compared with prices in Australia. Which is a good thing because, like most girls, I have a major shoe fetish.

Changing countries has been an exciting adventure. And it has also given me some new insights, especially about what it means to be a child of God.

Just by looking at me, you don't know my home country. But when you get to know me—when you hear me talk—you know I'm from a different place.

It's the same for Christians. Others can't tell by our outward appearance what we're like inside. It's when they get to know us—when they hear us speak and see how we live our lives—that they see we're coming from a "different place" than the rest of the world. If they like what they see, maybe they'll want to "go" there too.

> They said to the woman, "First we believed in Jesus because of what you said."
>
> —JOHN 4:42

God,
Help me live my life in a way that helps lead others to you.
Help me be your ambassador to the world. In Jesus's name,
amen.

You are a child of God, a person so loved and cherished that God wants to keep you around forever! Remember who you really are, inside and out, in everything you do.

insideout

{ write from the heart }

What do others see in you that makes them curious about the source of your joy, strength, and character?

_____

_____

_____

_____

_____

_____

_____

_____

_____

_____

_____

_____

_____

_____

_____

_____

EXCELLENCE

{kimiko soldati}

Kimiko Soldati grew up dreaming of being an Olympic gymnast, but when she endured a knee injury at fourteen, many people thought her dream would die. They didn't know Kimiko! She switched from gymnastics to diving and kept her eye on an Olympic goal.

Despite the devastating loss of her mother to breast cancer, Kimiko excelled on diving teams throughout high school and college and won a national title during the NCAA championships in 1996. In 1999 Kimiko became the first female in U.S. diving history to qualify for the finals in all five events at the national championships.

Between 2001 and 2004 she won another national championship and a silver medal at the World Cup. At the Goodwill Games in 2001, Kimiko won a bronze medal on the 3-meter springboard, an event the media had said was the least likely for a U.S. medal. Through hard work and training, Kimiko qualified to compete in the 2004 Olympic Games. Unfortunately, a shoulder injury prevented her from performing as she had hoped. Still, just becoming an Olympic athlete had been a dream come true for her. She came home with no medals—but plenty of joy.

Today Kimiko is married to Purdue University diving coach Adam Soldati and enjoys being a full-time mom to their toddler son, Blake.

{striving for excellence}

i didn't grow up knowing about God, didn't know I could have a personal relationship with Jesus. And even after I became a Christian as an adult, I didn't really understand what that meant.

One day I was reading a book by Christian athletes talking about "letting go and giving it all up to God." I didn't get it. Give what to God? Let go of what?

Maybe I dozed off. Maybe I prayed. Somehow an image came to me, like a movie rolling through my brain:

I'm underground, digging a tunnel with my fingers, trying to get where I want to go. Dirt is flying, my hands are sore, my back aches. I'm miserable.

Then I realize someone's standing by me. Wow! It's Jesus. "How ya doin', Lord? 'Scuse me. I've got work to do." I keep digging.

But I'm so tired. My fingers are bleeding, and the work is going so slowly. Then I notice Jesus is holding a shovel. I don't really like the idea—after all, I *could* do it with my own hands—but reluctantly I take the shovel. *There. I've accepted help. Are you happy?*

Using the shovel, I keep digging, but soon I'm too exhausted to keep going. I lean on my shovel, defeated. I can't do it. It's too hard.

Huh? Jesus is saying he wants me to give him the shovel. Whoa! I'm totally freaked out. "I don't *want* to give it to you, Jesus," I say. "What if you don't take me where I want to go? What if I want to be here but you take me *there*?"

He doesn't try to talk me into it. He just comforts me. Lets me know he's not leaving. Finally I lay the shovel in his hands. Finally I let go.

What a relief! What freedom! Suddenly I understand. I get it . . . because I gave up and gave control to Jesus. From now on, he'll do the digging, and I'll follow where he leads me. I know I can trust him with my shovel.

—Kimiko Soldati

You are my place of safety and protection. You are my God and I trust you.

—PSALM 91:2

a perfect 10, no matter what

there I stand on the platform, high above the water. Body poised. Focus sharp. Ready.

If you and I sat together looking at the photos and videos taken during my years as a dedicated competitor on national and Olympic diving teams, we would probably see some very different things. Seeing my muscular body, my rock-solid focus, and my accomplished moves, you might think I was supremely confident as I stood on that platform. Prepared, practiced, and in control.

I used to look at the old photos and see a nervous young girl, desperately trying to project a fake image of excellence.

Oh, I was prepared, and I had practiced; those parts of me were totally genuine. I knew what I had to do to win.

The problem was, I didn't know what I would do if I *didn't* win. My self-worth was completely tied up in what I could do, what I could achieve. I was consumed with excellence, with making each dive perfect—or as close to perfect as humanly possible.

Because if I didn't perform flawlessly, I wouldn't just mess up a dive. *I* would be a mess. *I* would be worthless. My whole sense of self-worth was tied up in what I could do, not in who I was.

When I became a Christian, it took awhile for that mind-set to change. It was sort of difficult to grasp the idea that to Jesus I was totally awesome whether I scored a perfect 10 or did a belly flop. Putting it another way, to Jesus I was to die for—literally!

He cares about *me,* not about what I can *do.* What an amazing concept, to be loved for just being . . . me.

So now I look at those photos and see them in a different light. There I stand on the platform, poised, sharp, ready . . . and loved, no matter what.

> Your goodness
> continues forever.
> —PSALM 119:142

Dear Jesus,
Thank you for loving me no matter how perfectly I fly and no matter how far I fall. I love you too, Lord, forever and ever. Amen.

If Jesus thought you were worth dying for, how can you think any less of yourself?

insideout

{ write from the heart }

Imagine yourself standing on a platform, waiting to perform in front of an audience of critical judges. What words would you use to describe your feelings? Next imagine yourself standing before Jesus, who loves you unconditionally. What words would you use?

_____

_____

_____

_____

_____

_____

_____

_____

_____

_____

_____

_____

_____

_____

_____

_____

a s an athlete, I have to spend a lot of time in the gym. For many years, when I was competing internationally, it was my home away from home. I spent the day there and at the pool. Basically I was doing the same things over and over: this much time on the elliptical trainer, this many crunches, this many reps on the weight machine. To keep from getting bored, I had to vary my routine, do different things on different days, change the order of the workout, or change what I did to work on specific muscle groups. I had a coach who held me accountable for sticking with the program. It still took a lot of determination and discipline on my part, but the results were worth the effort.

Spiritual training works the same way. To get to know God better, I spend time with him. Lots of time. *All* my time. I make him a part of everything I do. But I work on specifics too: I try to be disciplined and devote part of my day—every day—to reading the Bible and studying his Word. I change up the order so the Word stays

> Let the teaching of Christ live in you richly.
> —COLOSSIANS 3:16

fresh in my life. I change what I'm reading, trying different translations or reading inspiring books by Christian authors who give new insights on Bible truths. Maybe I think I know those stories inside and out— but as I see what *they* see in the passage, I learn a lot.

When I get lazy and let my "spiritual workout" slide, I can tell right away that something is different. My thoughts tend to drift into areas they shouldn't go. I may be less sensitive to others' needs . . . and less motivated to do what's right when it's not the easiest choice.

That's when I need to head back to the *Gem*, to God and his Word, to keep my life in shape.

Dear God,

You are my coach, my teammate, and my audience. Thank you, Lord, for helping me strengthen my spiritual muscles so I can use them to bring others to you. Amen.

being accountable to someone helps us stick with our improvement plan. Spending a quick moment with a friend each day to share a Bible passage and pray together is a great way to strengthen your friendship—and your kinship as children of God.

insideout

{ write from the heart }

Record your favorite Bible passages here. Write them out in different Bible translations as a way to change up your "exercise" routine as you read and remember them.

trying again . . . together

before I knew Laura Wilkinson as a friend, I knew her as my toughest competitor. When our paths crossed at national diving competitions, winning usually meant I beat Laura—and losing meant she beat me.

Then came my first Goodwill Games, an international competition. As two of the top divers in the country in 2001, Laura and I were both on Team USA. Suddenly the former diving competitors were teammates!

When we got to the games, we learned that, as the host country, Team USA got to enter an extra team in an event we hadn't planned on—synchronized diving, which involves two divers performing the exact dives in unison.

Our coach explained the opportunity to his team of divers. The divers looked at each other. Laura and I caught each other's eye. "We'll do it," we said.

We had never dived together, only against each other. But we quickly threw together a plan and performed our synchronized dives in competition, in front of the whole world.

There's something special about synchronized diving. You're nervous, as always, but somehow you feel less pressure diving together than when you dive alone. You're sharing the spotlight . . . or, in our case, the embarrassment.

> Let us run the race that is before us and never give up.
> —HEBREWS 12:1

We came in dead last.

Some people might have thought we made fools of ourselves. But we saw it as a new beginning. We loved diving together, and we kept at it. Eventually, we won medals in synchronized diving, and best of all, we developed a solid friendship that has been a blessing to both of us.

When you're nervous about trying a new opportunity, a challenge that might bring glory (or embarrassment), remember that you're not alone in doing what's good. God's right there with you, and, win or lose, he'll be your invaluable friend and supporter—forever.

Dear Jesus,
Thank you for creating in me the courage to accept new challenges—and giving me good friends who see me as a winner, even when I fail. In Jesus's name, amen.

there was only one perfect Christian—and he walked on water and rose from the dead! No one can compete with the Lord's example—and no one should try.

insideout

{ write from the heart }

What opportunities and challenges are in front of you right now? What can you do to gather courage so you feel confident about diving in?

_____

_____

_____

_____

_____

_____

_____

_____

_____

_____

_____

_____

_____

_____

_____

_____

_____

the trap of being the best

throughout my life I always thought I had to be the best: the best student, the best athlete, the best daughter, the best friend. You name it, I wanted to be the best at it. I drove myself crazy, always trying to do better than everybody else. (I probably drove a lot of other people crazy, too, in the process!)

It's good to have goals, and it's fine to work hard to achieve them. But if you're like me, you need to step back now and then and ask yourself, *Why am I doing this?* And even more importantly, *Who am I doing it for?*

Too often, girls give in to the pressure to be the best—without realizing where that pressure is coming from. Sometimes it comes from destructive thoughts and unrealistic desires. For many girls (including myself) the pressure to have the "best" body can become more important than staying healthy.

But when I realize where that pressure is coming from, I have to see it's not com-

ing from God. He would never pressure me to treat my body in a way that isn't healthy.

My "best" goal in life needs to be simply to please God, to make sure everything I do honors him. Whenever I feel pressured to achieve worldly results, I stop and ask myself: *Am I feeling this pressure because I want to please man or to please God?*

The best answer is a no-brainer. Instead of letting myself be trapped by others' expectations and pressures, I need to focus on what God says about me and wants for me: nothing but *his* best.

> If you do anything,
> do it all for
> the glory of God.
> —1 CORINTHIANS 10:31

Father God,
When worldly pressures mount, help me use them to press closer to you. In Jesus's name, amen.

the goal of a godly girl: bring glory to the One who waits for us beyond the finish line.

insideout
{write from the heart}

List the pressures you're feeling now to be "the best." Beside each one, write the source of the pressure. If you can't write Jesus's name beside something on your list, cross it out!

_____

_____

_____

_____

_____

_____

_____

_____

_____

_____

_____

_____

_____

_____

_____

_____

_____

letting go . . . and getting back

I crashed at the national championships in 2002. In a dive from the 10-meter platform, I hit the water in a backward-C. Seeing my head almost brush the back of my legs, the audience gasped. People thought I had broken my back.

Fortunately, I *didn't* break my back, but I did have to undergo surgery on my shoulder—the same shoulder that had already been operated on twice. During the year I worked to recover, every day was full of pain. But the 2004 Olympics were less than twelve months away, and I was determined to qualify for the team. Competing in the Olympics had been my dream since childhood.

Then came the day when I *couldn't* keep going. The pain was too great. Just eight months before the Olympic trials, I had to have another operation—which meant I had to give up my dream. *Poof!* It was gone. I couldn't possibly recover from surgery and then work my way back in time to qualify for the Olympic team.

God and I had a talk. Well, actually, I did all the talking: "Lord, if this is your plan, I'm okay with it," I prayed. "It's hard. But I'm giving you my dream. I'm letting it go. I know that if I'm not supposed to do this, it means you have a bigger, better dream for me in your plan. I'm just going to do my best to get strong again, and whatever happens, if I know it's what *you* want, then I want it too."

> Crying may last for a night, but joy comes in the morning.
> —PSALM 30:5

After surgery, I went through rehab, and I got stronger. I started diving again, but my timing was off. Still, I was at peace. I just kept working, practicing, and praying, thanking God that the pain was gone.

At the Olympic trials, Laura Wilkinson and I failed to qualify in synchronized diving, the event that was supposed to have been our ticket to the Olympics. But we both ended up winning our individual events and making the Olympic team together after all.

Yes, I went to the Olympics. No, I didn't win a medal. But just being there was my dream come true. I had given up my dream to God, completely at peace with whatever happened, and he gave my dream back to me.

Heavenly Father,
With you all things are possible. Help me to always remember that! In Jesus's name, amen.

More than anything in the world **around** me, I want to feel God's love and guidance **within** me.

insideout

{ write from the heart }

What impossibility could you give to God right now, exchanging
your burden for the peace of knowing you're living in his will?

_____

_____

_____

_____

_____

_____

_____

_____

_____

_____

_____

_____

_____

_____

_____

_____

_____

SURPRISED BY GOD'S PLAN

{ayiesha woods}

Ayiesha Woods was born in Long Island, New York, but lived in Bermuda, her parents' home country, for the first eight years of her life. In 1987, her family moved back to the United States. Her parents divorced in 1989, and during a two-year period in her teenage years, Ayiesha traveled with her mother and stepfather while they worked in an itinerant ministry.

Ayiesha grew up loving music and wrote her first song, "God Gets All the Glory," when she was twelve years old. She participated in musical groups throughout her high school years. Her performances in churches and other settings eventually led to her first independent solo project, *What You Do to Me*, in 2002. The record earned honors from the Caribbean Gospel Music Marlin Awards and caught the ear of popular Christian artist and record producer Toby McKeehan, known as tobyMac, who signed Ayiesha with his Gotee Records label. In 2006, she recorded the album *Introducing Ayiesha Woods*, which was nominated for Grammy and Dove nominations in 2007.

Today Ayiesha lives in Texas. With the help of her younger brother, Donald, she travels the country performing her music.

{surprised to be alive}

When I was born, my parents named me Shontae. But within a few days of my birth, I was diagnosed with a rare, fatal blood condition. The doctors told my parents there was no hope for me, and they should prepare themselves for my death and make funeral arrangements. There was no way I could survive, they said.

But my mother wasn't ready to give up just because some doctors told her it was hopeless! She starting praying and didn't stop. She promised God that if he would let me live, she'd give me back to him.

Well, that was more than twenty years ago, and (this probably won't come as a surprise to you) I'm still alive! Shortly after my mother began her prayers, the doctors checked my blood again and were surprised to find no trace of the fatal disorder. When there was no hope for my survival, God miraculously healed my body.

Because of that miracle, my parents promptly changed my name from Shontae to Ayiesha, which means life.

I grew up hearing this story, knowing that (in more ways than one) I am God's child and that he has a plan for my life. When I was twelve, I put my faith in Jesus as my Savior, personally confirming the belief my parents had always held *for* me until I was old enough to claim it as my own.

I am constantly amazed and thankful to see how God has worked his plan in me to create the tapestry of my life. As my relationship with him has grown, so have the gifts and abilities he has invested in me. I'm so grateful to him!

—Ayiesha Woods

> *All the days planned for me were written in your book before I was one day old.*
>
> —PSALM 139:16

surprised by worship

We all worship God in different ways. In the church where I grew up, worship was a solemn ritual that included reverent silence as a sign of holy respect and intense love.

We sang orderly, traditional hymns accompanied only by a piano; the hymn-singing was my favorite part of the service. Dancing in church was unheard of, and clapping our hands or shouting out affirmations during worship would have been considered distracting and out of order. Everything was very formal and focused on dignified reverence. For many years, it was the only kind of worship I knew.

> Sing a new song to the LORD; sing his praise everywhere on the earth.
> —ISAIAH 42:10

Then came the day when I was invited to a different church service, and I was amazed to find myself surrounded by worshipers shouting out to God with earnest praise, singing with their hands raised high and clapping to the music.

I'd never known such freedom in worship existed, and I soaked it up like a thirsty traveler crossing the desert. Those people let their love for God show in a rather wild and rambunctious way that I loved. I was swept up by the experience, and after that, there was no going back to the quiet, reserved kind of worship I knew as a child.

For someone who loved to sing—loved all kinds of music and loved expressing myself through songs—it felt wonderful to let loose all the boisterous, hand-clapping feelings for my Creator I'd held in restraint for so long.

Perhaps you grew up in a loud, charismatic church and one day found yourself in a quiet, ordered service that suddenly brought you into God's presence in a way you'd never experienced before. The thing is, God made each of us different. It's just a guess, but I believe he loves different kinds of worship, just as we do. Whether it's quiet, reverent hymns or rafter-rattling praise songs, he loves to hear his children's voices singing to him.

Dear God,
No matter how I lift my voice to you in praise, you smile down on me from heaven and bless me with your loving presence. Thank you, Lord! Amen.

Each in our own unique way, we praise God and show our love for him. As we worship him, others may notice how loving God makes a difference in our lives.

insideout

{ write from the heart }

What kind of worship brings you closest to your Creator? Describe
the service you would design to include all your favorite ways to
praise and show your love for him.

_____

_____

_____

_____

_____

_____

_____

_____

_____

_____

_____

_____

_____

_____

_____

_____

_____

hope in hard places

for a while when I was a teenager, our family moved from place to place as my parents answered various invitations to preach the gospel. Each stop brought a different living arrangement. We lived with strangers here—and family members there. Sometimes we had a house; sometimes we stayed in a hotel for several weeks.

I respected my parents' work but didn't understand why my life couldn't be like a normal teen's. Changing schools, not having much money, having to say goodbye to friends . . . it was all very difficult.

But now I look back and see that God was doing something amazing in me during that time of itinerant ministry. For one thing, he was working on my character.

I met teenagers whose situations were much worse than mine. I met people who used the gifts God had given them in amazing ways. And I saw people who ignored the talents God gave them and constantly complained about their situation.

I didn't want to be like those complainers, but the truth was, I thought God had given me the short end of the stick, constantly uprooting our family. Now I see that he was giving me something to write songs about! I had to experience the pain and discomfort of emptiness, brokenness, and despair before I could write about those things in a way that connects honestly with others who've also been in hard places.

> "I know what I am planning for you," says the LORD. "I have good plans for you, not plans to hurt you. I will give you hope and a good future."
> —JEREMIAH 29:11

Maybe you're in a place right now where you're frustrated, lonely, close to despair. I've been there, honey! And I want to remind you that God has a plan for you. Someday—maybe tomorrow!—you'll have opportunities to use what you're experiencing today to share Christ's love. Then it'll be your turn to reach out and say, "I've been there, honey! I understand."

Father God,
When I'm feeling down, help me to remember that you have good plans for my life. I cling to your promises, Lord! In Jesus's name, amen.

We can choose to let hard times swallow us up—or push us upward, ever closer to God.

insideout
{write from the heart}

What past difficulties have had a lasting impact on your life?
Describe how God has used a challenging time in your past to make
you more Christlike today.

_____

_____

_____

_____

_____

_____

_____

_____

_____

_____

_____

_____

_____

_____

_____

_____

open and closed doors

Under my bed there's a flat, black box containing the steppingstones that led to my musical career. What are they? Fifty or so cassette tapes of song ideas and snippets I recorded throughout my growing-up years.

> Ask, and God will give to you. Search, and you will find. Knock, and the door will open for you.
>
> —MATTHEW 7:7

There's nothing fancy about the music on those tapes. It's just plain ol' Ayiesha, sitting in a bedroom with the karaoke machine playing and the tape recorder running. I recorded one harmony on top of another and sang, without any instruments, the words and melodies that had come into my head.

Every now and then I drag out the box and listen to the tapes, giggling at how young and immature I sounded. Yet I'm amazed, too, to hear some of the original concepts that today are part of my professionally produced albums. Those ideas that first occurred in a young girl's head are now part of the dream-come-true I'm living as an adult.

But it wasn't a straight shot from singing alone in my bedroom to performing on stage in large arenas. I laugh now, remembering all the times my parents volunteered my services in little church programs and informal gatherings—"Ayiesha will sing a song for you!"—whether or not I wanted to at the time.

After high school, I wasn't planning to study music in college. But God seemed to close all the other doors. Then when I applied to music business programs, what do you know? Those doors opened to me. And the next thing I knew, I was completing that first album on Toby McKeehan's Gotee Records label. It seemed obvious to me that I was moving in the direction God intended.

Best of all, God came along with me! As my personal relationship with Jesus has deepened, my music has improved—because it's all about him. He has constantly surprised me with the way he continues to open doors for me and direct my steps.

Dear Jesus,
When you close a door in my pathway, help me see the new direction you're leading me. Amen.

there's no such thing as failure, really—only successful learning experiences.

insideout

{ write from the heart }

Describe your dream for the future. How will you know if you're following God's lead?

_____

_____

_____

_____

_____

_____

_____

_____

_____

_____

_____

_____

_____

_____

_____

_____

_____

_____

_____

God's blessings in surprising places . . . and people

i absolutely love traveling, especially on a music tour. I love the airplane flights and the overnight bus trips. Believe it or not, traveling by bus is sometimes even better than flying. After all, the "bus" is actually a motorhome, and those bus bunks are so comfortable! I love falling asleep after a concert in, say, Omaha and waking up the next morning in Tulsa, ready to go to work again.

The traveling is fun, but the very best part is knowing I'm being obedient to God's call on my life. I'll never forget the girl who came up to me after a show in Houston and said she'd been considering suicide and happened to hear my song "Happy" on the radio. As simple as the lyrics are, they spoke *life* to her, she said. Then the DJ mentioned our upcoming show, and she had come to share her story with me.

Even though my prayer has always been that my music would point people to Jesus, I remember feeling a little surprised that God had actually used *me* to bring such a blessing.

It felt the same way when a man from a prison ministry told me after a show in Florida that he had introduced my music to an inmate on death row—and how it had brought the young man a sense of freedom and peace.

Amazing!

We've all been blessed by someone in a surprising place—I know I have. A smile from someone in a long line at the airport security checkpoint, or a kind word from a

> Many people will praise God because you obey the Good News of Christ— the gospel you say you believe—and because you freely share with them and with all others.
>
> —2 CORINTHIANS 9:13

server in a restaurant, a compliment from the clerk at the discount store, or a polite gesture by a stranger in an elevator—even the smallest things can be blessings in a hurried day.

We never know how we affect each other. You may not even realize a blessing is happening—for you or for another person. But later you look back and see that God was there as blessings were exchanged.

God is so amazing! I think he gets a kick out of seeing us discover his presence in unexpected places and feel his love coming to us through people we don't even know. Watch for those blessings in unexpected places—around the next bend in the road or behind the next smile. And be prepared to be surprised.

Use me, Lord! As I travel through each day, help me connect with others in a way that brings them closer to you. I offer myself to you. Amen.

insideout
{write from the heart}

Describe who—or what—has been an unexpected blessing in your life this week. How have you been an unexpected blessing to someone else?

_____

_____

_____

_____

_____

_____

_____

_____

_____

Watch for God's blessings every day. Or, even better, **be** a blessing to someone else.

_____

_____

_____

surprised to be worth so much

We were on a three-week tour through Europe, and midway through the trip we found ourselves in Norway with a pile of dirty clothes. We asked about doing some laundry and were told to just give it to the clerks at the hotel's front desk, and they would take care of it. What could be easier?

The next afternoon, our clothes were returned to us, freshly washed, dried, pressed, and folded. And with the clean clothes came a bill—for $766! For two loads of ordinary laundry!

> God loved the world so much that he gave his one and only Son so that whoever believes in him may not be lost, but have eternal life.
>
> —JOHN 3:16

We were dumbfounded. I asked if there might be some mistake, but no, that was how much we owed. After all, someone pointed out, we were in a city with one of the most expensive costs of living in the world. With that kind of laundry bill, I could believe it! We could have come back home to America and bought a washer and dryer for that much money—plus a year's supply of detergent!

Later, when I was thinking about that incident, I suddenly remembered someone else who had paid a high price for something ordinary. I remembered Jesus and the high price he had paid—death on a cross—for something ordinary: *me*. And *you*.

We get "dirty" making mistakes; we can't help it. The Bible says we're *all* sinners (see Romans 3:23), and the price we owe for our sin is death (see Romans 6:23). But Jesus, God's only Son, paid an extraordinary price for us ordinary people. He loved us so much, he died in our place. An old hymn says we were "washed by the blood of the Lamb."

What a high price he paid for us. And what a priceless gift he gave us: eternal life with him in heaven when we acknowledge what he did for us. He must think we're something special!

Dear Jesus,
Thank you for paying such a high price for me. Lord, help me live my life in a way that acknowledges my great worth to you—and honors the priceless gift of your love. Amen.

When we fill our hearts and minds with our love for God, when our "inside lives" revolve around him, our "outside lives" can't help but show how much we're worth to him.

insideout

{ write from the heart }

How does it make you feel to know the Son of God paid the
ultimate price for you? Describe how you show your gratitude for
that gift in your daily life.

_____

_____

_____

_____

_____

_____

_____

_____

_____

_____

_____

_____

_____

_____

_____

_____

_____

{notes}

{notes}

{notes}

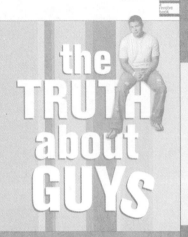